"No Dear, That's a Pheasant- We're Peasants"

We're Peasants"

Sonia Kurta

Published by

MELROSE
BOOKS

An Imprint of Melrose Press Limited
St Thomas Place, Ely
Cambridgeshire
CB7 4GG, UK
www.melrosebooks.co.uk

FIRST EDITION

Copyright © Sonia Kurta 2012

The Author asserts her moral right to
be identified as the author of this work

Cover designed by Jeremy Kay

ISBN 978-1-907732-52-2

Printed and bound in Great Britain by:
Mimeo Ltd, Huntingdon, Cambridgeshire

FSC
www.fsc.org
MIX
Paper from
responsible sources
FSC® C019549

In memory of Moira
'resting bricks'

Contents

Introduction

One of my earliest memories was going down to the end of our road and running across to see if some pigs had come up to that end of their field. We would scratch their backs and talk to them, which everybody enjoyed. On one of our walks we would pass a small paddock. In the weeks coming up to Christmas, several huge stag turkeys would be strutting about there. I found them both frightening and ridiculous. When they gobbled, it both looked and sounded as if they were gargling with marbles – and what was that weird appendage looking like an overblown earthworm, which hung over their beaks? What on earth was that in aid of?

Although there were several farms in the parish, the above was my sole direct contact with farming at home at that time. Our lifestyle was typically suburban. My father was a pharmacist and, in common with a high proportion of the wage earners, he commuted to London by train. To my knowledge, none of his family had ever had any connections with farming. It was rather different with my mother. Although her immediate family were not farming, she had several uncles and cousins who had farms in areas such as Bourton-on-the-Hill and in the Vale of Evesham. She told me that when one of the uncles had had a good day at the market, he was inclined to imbibe too freely. This was no problem. He was loaded up, the mare would be given a slap on her rump, and she would deliver him safely home, snoring contentedly. Transport nowadays can't do that, even with the most up-to-date Sat Nav system.

Another uncle went into partnership with his landlord to build lime kilns. They did very well until one of the workmen failed to follow instructions. He was overcome with fumes and was found dead.

When my mother was eleven years old, her mother was seriously ill. My mother and her brother and sister were sent to stay with relatives for a few months. Mother went to her Uncle Joe Spieres at Defford. They had a mixed farm in those days, and my mother was fascinated by everything that went on. The Spieres were a large family, and the young people had a donkey and cart. One of the older girls took my mother with her when she drove the donkey to the blacksmith to be shod. This upset the animal, and on the way home he bolted, the cart turned over and threw them off into a ditch. One day my mother heard the cowman say to her uncle, 'That cow Daisy is ready to go to the bull.' My mother ran indoors and said, 'Auntie, Auntie, why has Daisy got to go to the public house?'

When my mother's parents retired they bought two or three acres of land in Hertfordshire, and built a bungalow on it, as you could in those days. They grew all their own vegetables and kept a fairly large number of chickens. More by accident than design, Grandad acquired several goats. When I stayed there I enjoyed helping Grandad, and quickly decided it was far more interesting than being at school. What finally precipitated me into farm work was the war.

In the middle of the 1930s, as Hitler started his takeover of Europe, it became increasingly obvious that war was almost inevitable in order to restrain him. My mother remembered that in the First World War the Zeppelins often aimed their bombs at the railways. As we lived not far from London, and I went to school by train, it was decided that I should be evacuated. So I was sent to live with two retired school teachers she knew. I was there when war was declared. It was a lovely sunny day on Sunday, September 3rd, 1939. My guardians sent me off to church that morning. As I was walking there, I was wondering what was going to happen. Would we all be dead in a few weeks?

The teachers had promised a friend she could come to live with them when she retired. Her retirement occurred after I had been with them for a few months, so they were then able to say there was no room for me. I had met a girl in my class who was living with her brother on their grandmother's small dairy farm. Their parents were in Birmingham, so they were also escaping air raids. I went to live on this small dairy farm in Minchinghampton, Gloucestershire, and enjoyed the farm life as much as my mother had on her uncle's farm.

My father was much older than my mother, she being his second wife. He died in the Spring of 1940, just before my fourteenth birthday. He had been running one of the two chemist shops he had in London, with a manager in charge of the other one. All the stock and paperwork was moved to the shop the manager was in charge of for the time being. One day in the following Autumn of 1940, the manager was on his way to work when a man asked him where he was going. He thought this was a strange question until he got round the corner. Where the shop had been was just a pile of bricks. It had received a direct hit. The other shop had had all the glass blown out, and anything moveable looted. My mother had lost her entire income. She managed by letting rooms to the bombed-out and, when the shop my father had run was repaired, that was let too.

It was not possible to continue my education as had been planned, but I was delighted and left school to work on the farm. As soon as I was old enough I joined the Women's Land Army. (An account of my experiences as a farm worker will be found in '*Charismatic Cows and Beefcake Bulls*', published by Old Pond Publishing of Ipswich.)

CHAPTER 1
Back to School

The Land Army was disbanded in 1950. I stayed working on a farm in North Cornwall until 1953, then I finally admitted that I would never have enough money to get a farm of my own. The most I could have hoped for would have been to run a poultry unit or manage a dairy herd. For a woman to be a farm manager in those days was unheard of.

I could have started a small poultry operation, but I would never have been able to work up any enthusiasm for them. My feelings for chickens were not, however, as extreme as that of one farmer who, on being asked why he didn't keep poultry, said, 'Because they give me the creeps.'

Cows have to be milked 730 times a year and 732 times each leap year. I had been there and, much as I like cows, had no wish to carry on into the years to come, being 'tied to cow's tail' as one well known journalist of the day put it.

The front door to farming being closed to me due to lack of cash, and the back door only leading to the kitchen, I decided to try the library door. In those days the Government actually thought that producing food was important. They therefore offered scholarships to the sons and daughters of farm workers, or bona fide farm workers with a minimum of five years' experience, providing their parents' income was no more than that of a farm worker.

Having done about eleven years' full-time farm work and my mother having a very small income, I qualified easily for the second category. At first I had an ambition to be a vet, but was told that as a female I would only be able to work with small animals. As my interest was with farm animals, I decided to opt to do a degree in Agriculture if I was awarded a scholarship. At the interview I was asked what I would do if I failed to get an award. I said I would most likely try to get a job shepherding in Wales. I had visions of riding a pony over the hills!

The great news came that I had been awarded a scholarship to enable me to study for a degree, providing I could satisfy the entry requirements. This necessitated taking A-levels, which I had to do off my own bat. In those days you applied to each University yourself. I started in alphabetical order: Aberystwyth, Bangor, missed Cambridge as being too posh. In 1953 Kings College Newcastle-upon-Tyne was part of Durham University. This was very lucky, because all the others simply sent me a brochure giving requirements. Newcastle took the trouble to pass my enquiries on to their admissions tutor. He wrote saying that if I could get A-levels in Biology, Chemistry and Physics or Maths, I would be able to go directly into the second year. This meant that if you did well enough in your second (final) year, you went on to do honours in the third year.

Talk about fools rushing in where angels fear to tread! I signed up at Kingston-on-Thames Technical College to take Biology, Chemistry and Physics. Not only had it been eleven years since I had left school, but this was a revision class of nine months for those who had already done two years at school! Biology I could do standing on my head, Chemistry was possible, Physics? OK, joining up bits of wire was great fun. Other practical experiments, fine, but physics equals maths. Finding the subject boring, I had ignored it at school. The first lecture we had was the mathematical proof of how a spherometer measures spheres. Lines and little letters in all directions; all a complete mystery to me. I cycled home thinking I was completely mad.

A young graduate, with a wife and baby to support, advertised to give maths coaching on Saturday afternoons. He was very patient. I was chatting to his wife after one session, while he ran upstairs to change to go to a formal dinner. He hadn't worn the suit for some time. We heard a cry of despair, and he came down to show us that the leg of the trousers had split.

We admitted we could see white skin every time he moved. No time to mend the split satisfactorily, he vanished into the kitchen. In a few minutes he was back again.

'Can you see my white skin now?' he enquired.

'No,' we chorused.

He pulled up the trouser leg to show what he had done, which was to apply a liberal layer of shoe blacking to his leg! Having a degree in maths can have some unexpected benefits!

I somehow struggled through Biology and Physics, but failed in Chemistry, so I signed up to retake it in a few months. In the meantime, looking for a part-time job, I went to work for a young man who ran a riding stables. He said he couldn't afford to pay me much, but would give me free lessons. As he had been trained at Porlock by Tony Collins, who trained the Olympic team, this was top class tuition.

As with all animals, the horses had great characters. Dinah was three-quarter bred, feisty, bay mare. She was in no way vicious, but had a great sense of humour. She would look over the top of her loose-box door and pull faces at you, pretending she was going to bite. She was not easy to ride, being so very lively. I could just about

3

manage her on a gentle hack, even then having difficulty to look after the children I might be in charge of. When she went hunting, we had to find somebody who weighed at least ten-and-a-half stone to weigh her down. She took off one day with my boss, jumping everything in sight. That was when he decided to take her to the Elephant and Castle sales. She made a very good price as a heavy hunter.

Another strange mare was called Celia. I always thought she treated me very unfairly, as she would be looking over the top of her loose-box door when I arrived early in the morning. Then she would start to yawn. We would then have a competition, and when the boss arrived I would be leaning on the yard broom yawning my head off, which did not give a good impression.

Celia had one or two other tricks. They may not have been deliberately designed to annoy, but they did. Most horses, when confronted by trees hanging twiggy branches, duck their heads. Not Celia, oh no! She would stick her head straight up, pushing the vegetation aside on her chin or throat. The first time she did this with me on board, I was ducking my head just as hers was coming up. I got a badly-bashed nose, while she just got sworn at, which she took no notice of whatsoever. If I had her out for exercise on her own, she didn't trust me to find the way home. She would insist on putting her nose right down to the ground, sniffing and snaffling like an oversized bloodhound.

One of the horses, and it might well have been Celia, discovered how to turn its loose-box light on. The switches were of the rotary type, and were on the walls outside the loose-boxes. The first time I arrived on a dark morning to find the one stable with its light on, I concluded that someone must have gone in the previous evening and forgotten to turn the light off. But the light shone out like a beacon and none of the yard lights were on. After it happened several times, we came to the conclusion that the occupant didn't like being in the dark, and had found out how to reach round and nibble the light on.

In the summer of 1955, having obtained the required entry qualifications, I was waiting to start my first year at Newcastle. When I was a small child, a retired Scots doctor had lived a few houses away. I used to love to visit him to hear his tales and watch his pet canary, waiting for it to land on his head. Another little girl from opposite would wait as eagerly as I did for him to go up to Scotland, as he always brought us each a box of Edinburgh Rock.

The old doctor had been dead for a good few years by 1955. However, he had a daughter who ran a small private school. It seemed that she had a friend who had an estate in the Kyles of Bute. Knowing I would be grateful for any offer of temporary employment, she asked whether I would like to work in the gardens until I went to college. I certainly would, so was told to phone the factor. His accent was such that I had difficulty in understanding it, but gathered that he was asking whether I had a sister who could come up with me. When I told him that I didn't, he asked whether my mother could come. I could just imagine her reaction if I had suggested that she bury herself for weeks in the depths of a wild countryside. I was wondering why he was so anxious for me to have a female companion. Did he think I needed a chaperone? It turned out to be a more prosaic reason, for he said, 'There's nay water in the hoose.'

I rather thought he was trying to put me off – didn't fancy being lumbered with some probably useless English girl. It later became an 'in joke' between my husband and myself. If we ever felt someone was trying to put us off doing something, we would look at each other and say, 'There's nay water in the hoose.'

As it turned out, I couldn't go to Scotland as I had to go to Newcastle for interviews. The first thing I noticed was that the buses were bright yellow. Most other things at that time in Newcastle were black. When I mentioned this, someone said that if I thought Newcastle was bad I ought to see Leeds. Dufflecoats were all the rage among students. Most of them fancied ones that started off cream, but I chose charcoal grey. That way it always kept its original colour, whereas the cream ones became the same colour as mine very soon.

Rag Week was at the start of the year. There was a competition between the Agrics and the Engineers to get top marks for their float. Our lads had taken 'Noah's Ark' as their theme. My contribution was to make curtains for the ark. I couldn't think of anything else to do. A life-sized elephant led our entry. Cleverly built out of wire netting on a large Fiat chassis, there was room inside for two lads. They had several churns of water and a stirrup pump. One student operated the pump while the other manoeuvred the elephant's trunk with string, down which the water came to spray the onlookers at intervals. The next year our Agrics built a large model of Bacchus. Guess where the water was coming out that time!

There were over thirty students in my year, of whom just four were women. These were still the days when a woman automatically gave up work when she married, unless the family was very poor, in which case she might go out 'charring' or take in washing. A few exceptional women carried on working at a career after they got married, sometimes in partnership with their husbands; but this was rare. When I went up for interview I was asked by an elderly professor why I wanted to take a degree when, as he put it, 'you will be getting married'.

I refrained from saying, as I used to tell the foreman in the Caerheys estate, that I had no intentions of getting married, as his reply had been, 'the chance would be a fine thing.'

I suffered an even better put-down while at Newcastle. As we came off the field at the end of a hockey match, when it was pouring with rain and blowing a cold wintry gale, I trotted along using one of our larger players to shelter behind.

She remarked, 'That's crafty.'

'Ah,' said I, rather pleased with myself. 'I am not as foolish as I look.'

She gave me a withering stare. 'That would be impossible,' she informed me. Served me right!

We four female students were all completely different. Only two of us were doing a degree in General Agriculture. My fellow student, Edith, was rather sophisticated. I didn't know her background, but she had obviously had experience in practical work as, after one exam, Professor McGregor-Cooper, who was the Professor of Agriculture, remarked that it was a strange thing but the girls had done better in the machinery exam than the boys. Some of the lads had had little practical training, although a year of such was needed before you could come to college. Edith married the manager of the college farms. I believe they went to Wales.

The third female student read Agricultural Zoology. Her father ran a large acreage near Hadrian's Wall. Elizabeth was quite short, but I have never met anyone who could walk as fast without seeming to make any effort. She had always had to walk three miles from home and back again to catch the school bus. 'Straight-laced' is, I suppose, the best way to describe Elizabeth. She was quite a well-built lass, and I asked her on one occasion why she was wearing her coat in class. She pursed her lips.

'I don't want the boys looking at my bosoms,' she said.

When Elizabeth got her degree she went off to New Zealand to teach, at first for five years. She came back to England for a bit, but soon returned to New Zealand. I assumed she was teaching at an

7

agricultural college, but she was on the staff of a well-known girls' school on the South Island, where she became head of the science department. In 1989, after my husband had died, I went to Australia to visit relatives. I had always wanted to go to New Zealand, so I went touring there for a month after leaving Australia. I stayed with Elizabeth for a few days, and she drove me across to The Hermitage and Mount Cook.

Elizabeth was eight or nine years younger than I was, as were most of the other students, so she would have been in her early to mid-fifties when I stayed with her. She had smartened up appearance-wise, very considerably, but she was still the staid Elizabeth of old. When I told her that nearly all the schools at home were now co-educational, she was very shocked. New Zealand matrons at that time did seem to be similar to our schoolteachers in the 1930's.

I wonder if Elizabeth had a premonition of her death. I asked her what she planned to do when she retired and she said she would most likely return to England. She had a lovely bungalow, but she would have needed about four of them to buy anything similar in the UK. Also, she had made no arrangements about a pension. Soon after Christmas the following year, I got a letter telling me that she had been driving a visitor on the route she had taken me. As there is so little traffic on those roads, many stupid drivers belt along in the middle of the road. Elizabeth, being Elizabeth, kept well to the left. My informant said that she had been killed instantly whilst her passenger had not been harmed.

The fourth member of our select group was Laila. In my ignorance all I knew was that she came from the sub-continent of India. Now I know that it was East Pakistan, now called Bangladesh. Laila had all the elegant grace that would be expected of a high-class lady, which she was. She always wore a sari, which she fixed at her waist with nimble fingers. However hard I tried, I had only to walk forward a couple of yards before it dropped around my feet.

Laila was not married when she came to Newcastle, but during the first summer vacation she returned home to be married. She told us that it took two weeks, during which time she sat in a corner with her head bowed, while her husband welcomed guests. Tradition dedicated that she gave the impression that butter wouldn't melt in her mouth, but nothing could have been further from the truth. She was the boss. If she felt a bit under the weather, she would ring her husband and demand that he came over. Mind you, it seems he was only too happy to do this. As a Muslim, alcohol was forbidden, so it seemed he felt free to indulge in a few beers in England. As you may have already guessed, Laila was far from the fragile innocent butterfly which her culture dictated she should assume. During the summer vacation we were all expected to undertake practical work according to the experience each of us had had. Laila was sent to work on the University Farms, but they had no idea what to do with such a delicate creature until they saw her rolling a churn full of milk across the yard.

It was not only physically that Laila seemed to be the picture of innocent perfumed femininity. We were allowed to work in our free time in the labs. One afternoon, Elizabeth, Laila and I decided we wanted to catch up on our work. Having the experiments set up, Laila climbed up onto the benches.

She marched up and down saying, 'Teach me some English swear words!'

Elizabeth's reaction was one of horror. 'Oh, Laila!' she said.

Laila was planning to return home when she had completed her studies, to concentrate on the cultivation of rice, and developing new varieties. She therefore needed all the material she could get on this subject.

The Professor of Agricultural Botany was an elderly Welsh man called Martin Jones. His claim to fame was that he had persuaded some long-suffering wheat plants to struggle on from year to year as he continually cut their heads off so that they could not produce seeds. In his charmingly lilting Welsh voice he would say, 'There is no such thing as an annual or a perennial.'

He would then draw a horizontal line on the blackboard to indicate ground level, several vertical lines below it to represent roots, vertical lines above to represent stems and leaves, then put another horizontal line through these to show where he cut them off. After a time he would look down at his wrist and say, 'I think we have had time enough now.'

Needless to say, he wasn't wearing a watch. The boys thought he was a waste of space. I liked his lectures for their entertainment value. However, he was pretty useless to Laila. She complained that he gave her references from the 1890s!

Another eccentric person was the lecturer in Entomology. He would come on field trips with us and spend two hours or so lying on his stomach, watching some bug battling its way through the vegetation. One afternoon he was showing us slides. He always wore a deerstalker hat, and this he placed, crown down, on the bottom shelf of the projector. One of the lads picked it up, and it was passed round for everybody to put their loose change in. He was such a vague individual that we were all sure he wouldn't notice, and be showered with coppers when he put his hat on. We were mistaken. He switched off the projector, picked up his hat, and carefully poured the cash into his hand, then transferred it to his copious jacket pocket.

'Thank you so much,' he said. 'It will buy sweets for my children.'

Clamping his hat on his head he stalked out, leaving the lads open-mouthed, watching their beer money disappear through the door.

The one thing we four girls had in common was that we took our studies seriously. This was to be expected, as agriculture was a very unusual subject for a female in those days, and you would only do it if you were genuinely interested. The males, on the other hand, were rather different. Some of them were very committed, but others didn't have to bother too much. Their fathers were prosperous farmers and they were guaranteed a living whatever happened. One of their main interests was boozing. They even had a drinking club with a special tie with a bull's head on it. I wouldn't have known about this, but one Saturday evening I went to a dance in the Student's Union. One young man asked me for a dance, and proudly announced that he had just been made president of the club. To do this, he had had to outdrink all the others. He was still on his feet and seemed little the worse for wear. Hanging on to someone and moving his feet about probably helped. One less fortunate competitor was found crashed out in the gents.

Another student, who always wanted to be top in everything, went missing from lectures. When I asked where he was, I was told that he was in hospital with a burst stomach ulcer. He looked white and very poorly when he returned, but he was so determined that he still got a First. After leaving Newcastle, it was years before I heard of him again. I was watching television one day and recognised him. He had had a planeload of Angora goats on the way from New Zealand when the bottom dropped out of the market, and the price plummeted faster than the plane could have crashed. He looked a bit sick then too.

Occasionally we were expected to attend lectures at the School of Botany. One day the professor unwisely commented that the agricultural students were not much in evidence. At the next lecture we were due to attend, the lads were all sitting in the front on bales of straw. They had crates beside them and, as the professor walked in, they released several upset, panicking cockerels, who flew squawking all round the lecture hall.

Rugby was the most popular sport in that area. When we went out on field trips, a considerable amount of time was spent practising lineouts whenever a suitable object could be found to serve as a ball. On the way back there was often a stop at a pub for a little refreshment. Having lubricated their larynxes, when they climbed back into the coach the lads would burst into bawdy songs. They were not very good vocalists, so you couldn't hear all the words, but you could get the gist of it. It was a good job Elizabeth and Laila, who were specialising, didn't have to come on these trips. Elizabeth would have sat bolt upright staring straight in front of her, while Laila would have asked them to tell her the words.

The agricultural students were always trying to get one-up on other faculties. There was a small area of lawn outside the Student Union. The Agrics used their knowledge of the use of nitrogenous fertiliser to very good effect on this bit of grass. In neat, bright green lettering, appeared the message: BALLS TO MEDICS.

CHAPTER 2
What Now?

What to do now? If we imagined that the long summer vacations were going to be a holiday, we quickly found otherwise. Hardly having breathed a sigh of relief and started to relax after exams, we were told what we were required to do for the next eight weeks. Those who had not had much practical experience were sent to do farm work. I was sent to the National Institute of Agricultural Botany at Cambridge. They were apologetic about digs. The only place available was with an eccentric lady many of the students apparently couldn't cope with. If she proved too difficult, and their attitude indicated that she would be, I would have to find my own digs. The lady in question lived just round the corner from the NIAB in Huntingdon Road. I knocked on the door with some trepidation. What witch or dragon would appear? She turned out to be a rather ordinary-looking person, stoutly built, with a bland flat face and grey hair in a bun. About fifty years old, I guessed. She couldn't have been much more, as her elderly mother lived with her. I never saw this lady, but I would hear them conversing in shrill, high decibels – about what, I had no notion. They were French. The old lady refused to speak a word of English until she was carted off to hospital, whereupon she wasted no time in making it known that she was cold.

My landlady was called Mrs Briggs; her husband was an English man whose subject was French, literature probably. He had obtained a Professorship at a Welsh college. Mrs Briggs naturally assumed she would be going to Wales with him, but he told her to stay in Cambridge to look after the house. Poor lady, she was very hurt. She said that she had given his students free tuition in French. She was at a loss to know what she had done wrong. Perhaps her temperament had worn him down. She would wave her arms about and say, 'I'm French, I'm emotional.'

I wasn't sure if emotional was the right word. She was more like a noisy engine, continuously running in top gear at full-throttle. The first time she called me I thought the house was on fire. If I expected a polite knock at my bedroom door if she wanted to come in, I soon found how wrong I was. She would burst in at full speed whatever state of undress I might be in.

Although Mrs Briggs had her funny ways, she was amicable and kindly, and I grew quite fond of her. There was only one thing that really annoyed me. Her green fingers. She would snatch the most unlikely, dead-looking bit of twig, thrust it into the ground, and it would seem to beam with pleasure, snuggle down and proceed to grow into a fine plant. Unforgiveable!

Students from all round the world were sent to do vacation work at NIAB. One young Austrian, he couldn't have been more than seventeen, was over in England because he had to pass an exam in English before he would be accepted at college to study agriculture. On the way over on the plane he was learning words such as 'cup and saucer'. Every evening he worked at his books, and the next day practised what he had learnt on us. After eight weeks he could hold quite a good conversation. We learned from him how they had acquired horses from Hungary (pinched them?) and how puzzled both parties were to understand each other. At first they couldn't find out how to make the animals move, and then how to stop them.

On several occasions some of us would go out for the evening together. On one of these outings we went to a local dance. I found myself sitting next to a man who had been dancing energetically and needed a rest. We got into conversation and enquired of each other what we were doing in Cambridge. He was interested when I told him my name and that I was studying agriculture. He said that one of his sisters was called Sonia, and that he had been farming at home. When I had been at Thriplow in 1946/7 we had often gone to dances where there were Polish soldiers, as they had a de-mob camp near. Eugene was rather different, as he originally came from the Ukraine. As this area had been taken over by the Poles when they drove the Bolsheviks back, he had been brought up as a Polish citizen, and so was called up when Germany invaded Poland. Stalin grabbed this part back after the war, so there was no going back. It was bad enough in Poland, which was under occupation, but easier to get news and later to travel back and forth. To make too many enquiries over the border could lead to trouble. One man he knew had managed to trace his mother, and she and her brother were promptly sent off to a concentration camp.

Eugene never did find out what had become of his family. He had cousins in Canada and a priest from his village had also gone there, but none of them ever got any news. He was lucky that he had not been born in Eastern Ukraine. It had been agreed that all ex-Polish army personnel who wished to stay in the UK could do so, and this included Eugene. Many of the Ukrainians who had been under the Communists had suffered so much that they joined up with the German army. To our shame, we returned many of them into the arms of Stalin, to almost certain death.

Eugene asked me if I would like to go with him on a coach trip to Southend. When we got there the tide was out. Miles and miles of mud, and not much else. Not a great start, but we had many interests in common, and I was very impressed by the fact that he had bought a house when he had only been in England for about six years. Mind, it was in a sad state when he got it – no bathroom, no electricity and he had to have two lorryloads of overgrown bushes and other rubbish removed before he could get in the back door. It only cost him the equivalent of three years on the minimum wage. It would now cost ten to twelve years at minimum salary. No wonder young people cannot buy anywhere to live.

As neither Eugene nor I were love-sick teenagers sighing over impossible goals, and we got on well and both had ambitions to run our own small enterprise of some sort, we decided we might as well be partners. In those days, no doubt to the surprise of the present generation, that meant getting married. As neither of us had a penny, we wouldn't be able to quarrel about one partner just being after the other one's fortune. We got engaged at Christmas, when I still had over a year before I would get my degree. We got married soon after I had taken my final exams, and I came to live in Cambridge.

Eugene wanted a Ukrainian Orthodox wedding. So we went to Notting Hill, where a priest lived, to make arrangements. These priests dealt only with their own countrymen, so did not bother to learn much English. I did not understand a word of what was going on, but learned from Eugene afterwards that, as the Ukrainians had no Church of their own at that time, the Church of England would allow weddings to be held in our Parish Churches. I had not lived at home for years so had never met our vicar. When we went to see him and put that suggestion to him, he threw a major wobbly. No way was he going to have an Orthodox service in <u>his</u> Church! So we had to apply to the Bishop of Guildford for a special dispensation. The vicar reluctantly climbed down providing that we had an Anglican service first, to be followed by the Ukrainian. So I have always said that I have been married twice. If people look surprised, I say well this was to the same man on the same day.

Eugene had told me a little about the Orthodox wedding ceremony. I understood that there were two best men and also that, at a certain part of the ceremony, crowns were held over the couple's heads. Eugene said that at home these had been made of gold with precious stones, but the ones which were being used for our wedding were replicas made of cardboard with coloured glass stuck on. In a way this was fortunate because they were much lighter. I had not been told that the crowns would be held over our heads for the whole of the ceremony and I had on a small headdress. So the man standing behind me could not really rest it on my head. I could feel his hands beginning to shake. Worse was to follow.

We were each given a lighted candle. Holding these, and followed by the faithful best men still holding the crowns over our heads, we had to process round the altar three times. Anglican churches are not designed for persons to go round the altar, so it was rather a squeeze. Afterwards my aunt told me that she thought I was going to set somebody alight with my candle. I would not have been at all surprised if I had, because I had a much greater worry on my mind. I had a short train on my dress and no idea that I was going to have to walk around, being followed at close quarters by someone trying to hold a crown over my head. I could feel his big feet treading on my gown and I was terrified that at any moment there would be a loud ripping noise and I would be standing in my underclothes. Fortunately no disaster took place, but I was amazed when people said what an impressive ceremony it had been.

Ukraine priest on the left, and vicar on the right

Rather than remaining in Cambridge, I would much preferred to have settled in the West Country. One of the farms on the Caerhays estate became vacant, and I would have liked to apply to rent it. Eugene was much more sensible than I was. He pointed out that we wouldn't be able to afford to stock it. In the long run it proved to have been the sensible thing not to rent, as we would no doubt have had more money in the bank when we came to retire, but that would have been eaten up by having to find somewhere to live due to the massive inflation in house prices.

Eugene had had enough of being tossed hither and thither, so we decided to stay in East Anglia. Being used to having hills to hold me up, looking over the flat landscape to the far horizon made me fear I would fall flat on my face, until I got used to it.

Having qualified as an agricultural economist, I started to look round for a job until we could scrape up enough funds to start our own business. I wasn't really prepared to commute to London, where I understood posts were available because agriculturalists prefer not to work in the City. The University of Cambridge at that time had a Farm Economics branch, attached to the School of Agriculture. It was completely separate from the Department of Land Economy, which in those days was still instructing the Honourable this or that how to manage their large country estates before it was realised that Inheritance Tax, and other changes, had destroyed that way of life for the vast majority.

Not knowing the correct procedure when applying for a University post, I simply walked in, introduced myself to the receptionist and asked how I might apply.

'Wait here a minute,' she said. I assumed she had gone to find the appropriate forms, which I would carry away, fill in, and that would be the end of my attempt. To my surprise, the young woman returned and told me that the Director would like to see me. Had I mentioned that my dissertation had been on the Marketing of Beef Cattle, I wondered? What a boring subject, you may think. Well, it fascinated me, especially when I came across J.R. Haldane's *The Drove Roads of Scotland*. On our field trips we would sometimes find ourselves walking along wide tracks across the hills, often contained within stone walls. Haldane told how in the 18th century drovers would take stock from Scotland all the way to the London markets, resting them for a time on the Norfolk pastures. Even with this recovery period, their average live-weight was only about 7cwt (356kg)! It seems that these drovers were so trusted that they would issue promissory notes to those they had bought the cattle from and these were accepted as currency by the local people.

Whatever it was I might or might not have said, it seems that I had arrived just at the opportune moment when the Department was looking for someone to work on the economics of beef production. I was taken on as a Junior Research officer, two years probation to start and then five year appointments thereafter. They had obviously learnt the pitfalls of life appointments.

At my interview they had taken it for granted that I had a car, or at least a driving licence, as I would have to visit all the co-operating beef farmers twice a year to collect data. I had a licence to drive a tractor or a motorbike, but had never had a car to take a test in. My lack of this accomplishment was greeted with astonishment, and I was told to pass my test pronto, and then I could use the Department car. This was a ropey old Ford, used by sundry students when they did vacation work. After a year or two its steering got so bad that I used to close my eyes when having encounters in narrow lanes.

The reasons for these visits were threefold. To give a service to the farmers by doing profit and loss accounts and other advice to them on the business side of beef production.

The second, and main reason, was to find which method of beef production paid the best under different circumstances, to be able to give advice. There were no desk computers in those days. For simple calculations we used calculators the size of typewriters. As the 'new boy', I was given one that jumped across the desk like a large frog as it worked. For more sophisticated work, we bought time on the computer, which was housed in a controlled environment in the Department of Mathematics. Only privileged operatives were allowed near it. We could only peer through the glass doors. It operated with punched tapes and we had one person trained to punch these. Three tapes for each assignment. 1) Date and job, 2) Program, 3) Data. Each tape was rolled and held together with a rubber band. Results came back on folded sheets about a mile long. We had our own expert to whom we all ran with problems, and who wrote some of the programs. One day I found him with yards of print-out round his feet saying, 'This just does not make any sense.'

He then started to examine the punched tapes. 'Oh, no wonder, the program tape has been wound the wrong way.' Someone must have dropped it, and then re-wound it the wrong way. I never really understood what I was doing with these calculations. People said it must be easier with the computer. It was certainly quicker, for example, with Linear Programming which showed how to get the maximum benefit from a given mix of inputs. I was told that the machine would do in 60 seconds what would take five weeks on a desk calculator. But you had to be careful with it. On one occasion it 'thought' it could make a small profit per acre by switching one item offered of feed for another for cattle under certain circumstances. It grabbed this with great enthusiasm. Fortunately it ran out of acres or would have kept going for ever.

The third reason for collecting input/output data from the farms, I kept rather quiet about. I made sure to include all the costs, because the Ministry of Agriculture used the results to argue with the N.F.U. at the February price review, which set the Deficiency Payments to be made. I had to get this information for beef production for East Anglia to the Ministry by January 1st. Christmas Eve would find me frantically working until the caretaker got tired of waiting and threw me out. The reason for this rush was that I had to wait for grazing animals to come indoors before I could go round the farms, in order to get all the data for the summer season.

After being taken to one or two farms by an experienced member of staff, I was left to do the rounds on my own, to collect the information we needed. For the reason mentioned above, it was well into the autumn before we could start going round the farms.

The winter of 1958/9, and subsequent years, seemed to be much more foggy than they are now. When it was cold and icy it was not a very pleasant experience driving along strange roads in the dark. There was no heater in the car, and in any case it would not have helped if there had been because I had to keep my side window open so I could see where I was going by looking out of it. On several occasions I had to stop and get out as I was not sure whether I was on the road or not.

It was usually daylight when I arrived on the farm. At first I didn't notice in which direction I was facing when I parked. Farmyards tend to have roads or tracks going in all directions. It was not until I had been embarrassed by having a whole household with lamps turning out to chase me when they realised that I was heading straight for their pond, that as soon as I arrived I always made sure to face the car in the direction I should take to leave.

In those days the A1 went through the centre of Stamford. After an especially foggy period I went to see a farmer who was a tenant on the Burghley estate. I remarked on how bad it had been and the man chuckled. He was a friend of the farm manager at Burghley House. The entrance that he used to get to his house was on the A1. On one of those foggy evenings he had been driving home on the A1. He had turned off towards his house, and had gone about a couple of hundred yards before he realised that all the nose-to-tail traffic had followed him.

'What did he do?' I asked.

'Oh, he just went up to the first car and said, "I'm sorry, old man, but this is not the A1, I'm on my way home" and drove off and left them to it.'

After the nightmare of the winter visits and then being stuck in the office the rest of the winter, the spring and summer visits were a joy. I saw some wonderful cattle, and some that were not so good. One mean old man had bought a bunch of heifers, and was boasting to me about what a bargain he had got. There was something about them I didn't like the look of and I was not certain he had got such a bargain. Sure enough he rang me up a few weeks later to say he was in trouble. It seems his 'bargains' were riddled with Coccidiosis. This was normally a dreaded disease in poultry. I had never heard of it in cattle before. The reason for ringing me, of course, was to try to get free advice to save paying a vet. I told him to isolate them, keep other cattle off any grazing they had been on, and get a vet pronto. Whether drugs could have got them back into condition at a reasonable cost, I have no idea.

If the farms we were visiting were more than fifty miles away from Cambridge, we were expected to get overnight accommodation – prices strictly limited. This suited me as I could usually fit in visits in the evenings, which was also convenient to the farmers. It was the days when socks were made mainly of wool, and wore out at an annoying speed. I used to fill up my case with Eugene's socks and sit and darn them in my free time. The ashtrays would be filled with bits of wool instead of ash. Usually I stayed at places recommended by other members of staff or where I had stayed before, and generally booked in advance. However, one summer evening I found myself in the back of beyond with no bed booked. In a small village I came across a pub run by a lady and her daughter. They said they had a room free, and I was just settling in when there was a knock on the

23

door. Two weary cyclists had arrived looking for somewhere to rest their aching limbs. Would I mind letting them have my double room? The daughter could move in with her mother and I could have her room. Fine by me. Unfortunately, nobody told the cat. I was just preparing to get into bed when I heard a slight 'plop'. There in the middle of the bed, having arrived through the small fanlight at the top of the window, was a large, fluffy feline. The poor thing was terrified. Instead of finding his friend to cuddle up to for the night, there was a weird stranger, who would most likely attack him. I have never seen such huge eyes. We looked at each other for about three seconds, then he turned and clawed his way up to the fanlight and struggled out. I have only recently learnt that a cat's heart normally beats at an amazing 180 times a minute. That poor animal's heart must have been jumping out of its chest.

The most extraordinary thing that occurred on one of these visits was on one summer evening when the sun was going down. It was my first visit to this particular farm. I drove into the farmyard to see three men standing staring at a blank wall. Before I had time to decide this might not be a sensible place to remain, and without any preliminary introduction, the farmer strode over and said, 'Come and look at this.'

So there were now four of us looking at a blank wall. After a short while one of the men said, 'Oh look! It's got one.'

What was happening was that the setting sun was shining on the wall, and flies were warming themselves on it. Wasps were catching them, holding them tight while they chopped off the flies' wings. You could see them fluttering to the ground. Then the wasps flew off with their prizes. I suppose they were food for their grubs.

It was decided to carry out a survey of beef farming in East Anglia to find out the methods being used, such as single suckling, beef from surplus dairy stock, and how fed and at what age sold. To do it, it was necessary to find out which farms had cattle. We were allowed to examine the June returns. As they had to stay on Ministry of Agriculture premises at Brooklands Avenue, we had to go to examine them there. They were locked in a cabinet to which we were given the key each morning, with strict instructions to take the key with us at lunch times. My assistant liked to have just half an hour so that she could get off early, whilst I went for a stroll round the Botanic Garden to get a bit of greenery to look at. So she would take the key. One day she got held up. Tired of waiting, I was wondering what to do when I noticed that the adjoining cabinet had a key in the lock. Thinking it could not possibly fit, I idly tried it. It opened the cabinet as easily as the one we were supposed to guard so carefully!

Having found which were the farms in East Anglia with cattle on them, I drew up appropriate forms and sent them off. There were about four sheets with tick boxes so that the farmer could indicate what system of beef production he was undertaking. I had made it as simple as possible, with a return pre-paid envelope enclosed. It would take no more than five minutes to deal with. I was very pleased to get over fifty per cent replying. One, however, puzzled me a good bit. Almost every single box was ticked. So I rang up.

'Tell me,' I said. 'Do you actually have a dairy herd and single-suckling herd and buy in store cattle?'

'No,' he said, puzzled.

'Ah,' says I. 'Do you by any chance have a small person around the place?'

'Yes, a small daughter.'

'Well, she has increased your stock no end. I hope you are paying her a good salary.'

He laughed and sighed, 'I must remember to lock the office door.'

The farmers who hadn't answered, I telephoned. This netted nearly

25

all of them. The few remaining I called on when I was in their area. One or two were unpleasant, just by being asked what were – to them – silly questions. I had discovered that they were much happier to co-operate when prices were low, in the hope of getting some advice. This I could often do. For one farmer who weighed his cattle, I drew a graph telling him exactly when to sell to get the best margin. Two heads are better than one, and an outsider could often see how a small change could make a big difference.

One strange holding I presented myself at was a few acres, surrounded by a rapidly expanding Chelmsford. On driving into the yard on a wet day, the first thing I saw was a dead calf lying in a puddle. The owner, as I suspected, was quite mad; way beyond eccentricity. I was greeted by, 'We don't like women, but now you're here you better come in.'

The place was filthy and, to my horror, he gave me a cup of tea. I pretended to be left-handed. At least that way, I reckoned, no-one else's lips would have been there. I felt sorry for the poor man. Years ago it had probably been a prosperous farm. He had refused to sell his last few acres to a developer and now had a compulsory purchase order hanging over him. As he was telling me about this, his aged father came tottering through the kitchen bearing his chamber pot. As I got up to leave, he gave me a book.

'You can borrow this,' he said.

It was the agricultural survey for the county of Essex – a survey undertaken for every county at the end of the eighteenth century. Absolutely fascinating. The writer was very impressed by the Welsh women who came with their drover husbands. They would buy a crop, probably soft fruit or peas or something similar, pick it, and then walk miles into town with as much as they could carry.

I was overawed by the intellectual gymnastics performed by some academics, but as time went on I developed a healthy disrespect for much of it. However I would not have had the courage of one young man. An open lecture was being given by some visiting VIP, and I attended. He put a great long equation on the board, and proceeded to discuss it without explaining what the symbols stood for. In his field perhaps some of them were conventional. Anyhow, I was quite out of my depth. Sitting at the rear, a student, whose skin colour political correctness does not allow me to mention but I should imagine came from West Africa, was obviously as lost as I was. With characteristic mischievous humour, he piped up, 'I think the "a" should be squared.'

Heads turned from the front rows. I hope his head did not roll the following day.

On another occasion one of my colleagues came into the office which I was sharing with a very pleasant young man called Brian. The first character started speaking reams of jargon to which Brian seemed to be able to respond. I sat there thinking, 'Now I know I am in the wrong job.'

After he had gone Brian turned to me and said, 'What was he talking about?' It seems that this person used to visit the Ministry of Agriculture. At first they thought what a clever man he was. Then they realised he was talking nonsense.

Another time we had a visiting economist who gave a lecture on milk production. We received his papers before the talk, and when I had unravelled it I discovered he was applying the concept known as 'The Theory of the Firm'. He conveniently forgot that for this to work it is necessary to have perfect knowledge and perfect competition. You cannot apply it in that simplistic way to the milk industry, of which he had no knowledge. I was waiting for more senior members of the university to question his conclusions but nobody said a word. I could only conclude they were so flabbergasted that words failed them. A pity, because he left thinking what a clever man he was.

There were cases of erroneous pronouncements or mistakes being made which, coming from a university, were accepted without question. Sir John Hammond was a very well-known animal husbandry expert. Sometime between the wars he had said that as families were now smaller, they would need smaller joints of meat, and he stated the weight lambs should be at slaughter. This figure was still being trotted out many years later in the 1960's. Farmers were complaining about the poor prices they were getting. Talking to butchers, I was told that the main demand was for chops. To get a decent chop they needed a much heavier lamb. Shoulders and legs could be cut in half. This indicates the danger of placing too much reliance on given advice without checking for oneself.

Trusting students doing vacation work to carry out their duties properly could also lead to trouble. The Farm Management section collected physical and financial data from farms in the farm management scheme, and results after analysis were returned to them. One year a whole batch of results were returned by farmers to say that the information had nothing to do with them. One crafty, lazy student had sat in his room in the warm and made up the figures! When we were at Newcastle we were told about a calf-rearing regime that had been developed recently by Cambridge University. If I remember correctly, it dealt with comparing the udder development and subsequent milk yields of calves reared by different methods of feeding. The conclusions were probably totally correct, but the means by which they were arrived at were somewhat dubious. The two students responsible for keeping the records lost them. In sheer panic they appealed to a member of the Farm Management team to help them out by suggesting what their records would have shown, which he did.

The gem was 'the fly who built a sugar beet factory'. Brian, with whom I shared an office, had been asked by a well-known magazine to write an article on sugar beet production. He had the galley proofs spread out on his desk, and asked my opinion of the layout. He had produced a dot map to show the location of each sugar beet factory. I noticed a dot over in the West Midlands.

'I didn't know there was a sugar beet factory over there,' I said.

Brian looked. 'Neither did I,' he said.

We looked at each other and burst out laughing. It was mid-summer. During her perambulations over the paper, a fly had deposited a fly blow. It was exactly the same size as the other dots! I assume that 'factory' was hastily removed from the map. Otherwise there could have been puzzled farmers in the region thinking to grow a few acres of beet, and trying to find a home for it.

CHAPTER 3
Eugene

Eugene at Home

At the beginning of the 20th century Philip and Stefanie Kurta were starting married life on their farm in Western Ukraine. Although their farm was small compared with many of those in the UK, it was the largest in their village. This was partly because Philip's brother had sold his land to them in order to train as a doctor. It was on some of the best soil in the world.

The young couple had six children, four boys and two girls. Eugene was fifth of these children, born in 1912. All indications were that they would be able to enjoy a quiet and reasonably prosperous life. True, a relation arrived home as an invalid, having survived a bayonet wound in the Russo-Japanese war, but this conflict had been many miles away. Then in 1914 the First World War broke out. The doctor brother was immediately called up. A report came that he had been seen being driven round to treat the troops on the Western Front. Typhus was rife, and presumably he succumbed to this, as he was never seen or heard of again.

Then came the Russian revolution. Not only Bolsheviks but many other factions with their own private armies popped up all over the place, some even issued their own currency.

One day when Eugene was six years old, he was getting under his mother's feet. To give him something to do, she sent him down to the river which bordered their land to see what the geese were doing. A ditch ran beside the path. It was a very hot day. The clear, cool water was too much of a temptation for a small boy. He jumped in to cool off. Splashing happily about, he was not immediately aware that he was not alone. He looked up - straight up the barrel of a rifle! The stranger, mounted on a horse, said something the child did not understand. He had heard the grown ups saying that an army was hiding in the woods nearby, so he waved an arm in that direction. That seemed to satisfy the man, who rode away.

Another day Eugene and his father were in their yard when a Bolshevik rode past. The two men began to argue. The Bolshevik threatened to shoot his father, who said "You'll have to shoot me in the back, then" and turned round and walked away. The Bolshevik rode on. At one stage, the conflicting armies were too close for comfort, so the whole family hid in the deep pit in the barn which was used for winter storage.

When things finally settled down, the Poles had driven the Bolsheviks out of Western Ukraine, so the Kurta family and their neighbours became Polish citizens.

Stefanie's brother had been a government officer when they were under Russian control. He naturally lost his job, although he continued to help people in a private capacity. Many of the people couldn't afford to pay him. Some gave him vodka instead. Whether this was the partial cause, it was not long before he died of tuberculosis. Stefanie's family seemed to be rather delicate, several suffering from respiratory diseases. A few years later Philip sent to England for a Singer sewing machine for one of the girls, as she was a keen needlewoman. One cold day, sitting at the sewing machine in a draught she caught a chill. This developed into double pneumonia from which she died. She was only twenty one years old.

Stefanie's brother's widow couldn't see much future for herself and her two boys so she emigrated to Canada. While things were still in a state of flux many people were on the move. The village cobbler was kept busy fitting their footwear with hollowed out heels into which they crammed all the gold they could muster.

After a relatively short time everything settled down into a normal pattern, the only difference being that the people were now under Polish rule instead of Russian.

The seasons came and went, reliably cold in winter and hot in summer. The children loved to pull off their boots when the spring came to run in the soft dewy grass. As soon as the ice was strong enough in winter, they strapped on their skates. A cartwheel had been put on top of a pole in the middle of the river. Ropes hung down which they hung on to while they spun the wheel round, then let go to see who could slide the farthest. A more usual use for cartwheels on poles was for storks to build their nests on. The storks were thought to bring good luck, so they were encouraged to build near your house.

The boys formed gangs to get into mischief and skirmish with rival gangs. One of their favourite tricks was to wait for an old man who drove a cart full of sugar beet past. The boys would put a string across the road, and hold it just high enough to knock the old farmer's hat off. When he got down to retrieve it, they would snatch the beet off his cart. It was not that they really wanted the beets. It was just the fun of seeing how annoyed the old man got.

At school Eugene was a bright pupil. The only ones to beat him were two Jewish girls. Their own school was too far away, so they came to the local school. Jews were not allowed to own any land in Poland. Perhaps the government was afraid that they would soon own all of it, with their single-minded ambitions. Early one morning a young Jewish boy walked past. Eugene asked him why he was out so early. "Father says I can't have any breakfast until I have sold something" he replied.

Over the next few years the only mishap Eugene had was entirely his own fault. He took a short cut across their neighbour's garden. The neighbour's dog took exception to this trespasser and knocked Eugene down. Not long after this the dog took exception to a policeman walking past, who promptly shot him.

There was a cinema in the nearby town where some of his cousins provided the entertainment for the audience during the interval between films. When he got a bit older they would sometimes allow Eugene to join them by playing the mandolin. He really wanted to play the guitar and spent summer evenings practising, sitting on a seat which his family had built under the shady tree near the back door.

Eugene at War

When Eugene reached the age of 21 he was called up for military service. He was the best shot out of his batch of recruits, and was given two weeks' leave as a reward. As he was leaving to return to his unit, his mother bade him goodbye, and said she did not expect to see him again. Her family frailty had reared its head. She died of bronchial asthma while he was away. She was 46 years old.

While Eugene was doing his military training Marshal Pilsudski died. Eugene was one of the soldiers who lined the route at his funeral. Military service completed, Eugene returned to the former routine. He persuaded his father to sell off a bit of land several miles from the farm, which could only be used for hay, and was more of a nuisance than it was worth. One of the ways they increased production was by planting up a new orchard.

Then in September 1939 Germany invaded Poland. Eugene had been out dancing until the small hours. As he wended his way homeward the uppermost thought in his mind was how he could discourage Maria who fancied him, to give his full attention to Anna. There was a card waiting for him on the kitchen table. It was his call up notice. He was to report to his unit immediately. If his mother had been alive she would have waited up for him, but the others were fast asleep. Eugene gathered up a few belongings, and left without disturbing them. When he turned to close the door behind him he never realised that he would never touch it again, or see or speak to any of his family for the rest of his life.

The young soldiers were put on trains to travel to the front. As they disembarked, German planes were waiting for them. Many were dead before they touched the ground, ripped apart by enemy fire. The survivors ran for cover. Eugene and his comrades were beside a road running through woods when they heard a tank rumbling towards them. Thinking it was a German tank, they were ordered to get ready to see what damage they could do to it with hand grenades. It was

Eugene on the right

not a German tank, it was Polish. The officer in charge was weeping broken heartedly. "We have been building up Poland for twenty years, and now our efforts have all been smashed" he lamented.

Soon it was obvious that trying to resist the German onslaught was useless. The order was given that it was "every man for himself" and that they were free to go home if they could get there. It was not long before Eugene and his companions came to a great, fast flowing river. There were horses running up and down the bank, calling for their masters who had deserted them. One of his comrades came up to Eugene mounted on one of these animals. "I'm going to try to get him to swim across" he said. "You'll drown, just look at it, it's impossible" Eugene told him and then pointed out a group of high ranking officers further up the bank, what we would call "Brass Hats". They will get a boat if anyone does, let's go and stand near them, and see if we can manage to get in it". Sure enough a boat appeared. Eugene and a few other soldiers helped to pull it in, and when the officers were aboard, push it off and jump in themselves. Half way across the boat stuck on rocks. A warrant officer ordered a couple of the soldiers out onto the rocks to push the boat off. Luckily Eugene was not one of the ones this man picked out. When the two who had been given the order were reluctant he drew his pistol and threatened to shoot them. They then clambered out. Having succeeded in refloating the boat, they were unable to scramble back quickly enough, and were left on the rocks in the middle of the river. Having succeeded in crossing the river, Eugene and his companions continued towards Rovno, which was about forty kilometres from his village. Having been a Boy Scout, Eugene knew that one directional guide was that moss grew on the north side of the tree trunks. What other methods they used to travel in the right direction seemed to have been successful. Any vehicles they came across they would use if they had any fuel left in them, until this ran out. One day they came across a house, and they knocked on the door to see if the householders would give them something to eat. "Of course we will" they were told "come in come in, but leave your rifles outside – we are Germans".

Eventually they approached Rovno. Coming up the road was a Russian tank with a 'Polish' officer perched on it shouting through a loud hailer. "The Russians are our friends" he was saying "hand over your rifles to them, and then they will arrange transport to take you all home." As Russian soldiers were lining the road, they had no choice but to do as he had told them. Walking on they asked some civilians what their opinion was of what they should do. The people said they were willing to give them civilian clothing, but then they would have no papers, which would mean big trouble if they were stopped. They were told that Polish soldiers had been going through all day, and it seemed to be all right, so Eugene's group decided not to risk discarding their uniforms.

When they reached the centre of Rovno they were rounded up and put on trains, which they were told, and hoped, would take them home. In any case they had little option, the Russians were armed and they weren't. The betrayal that was taking place Eugene found very difficult to cope with. His family, as Ukrainians, not Polish by birth, had lived under Russian jurisdiction for many years, they even bred horses for the Russian army. He had regarded the Russians as brothers.

Of course, the Communists had no intention of helping the Polish soldiers. Hitler and Stalin's pact meant that these men were now prisoners. The trains were driven further and further east into the area of Ukraine under Communist control. At one point the train slowed down enough to enable some of the men to jump off. Eugene decided not to try this, partly because he was engaged in playing cards! The men who jumped off may or may not have done the wisest thing, nobody ever heard. For the next few months, during the winter of 1939/40, the prisoners were set to work breaking stone which contained iron ore for smelting. The local Ukrainians tried to help to make life a little more tolerable, but couldn't do much. They had plenty of money, but nothing to spend it on.

At this stage the prisoners were able to receive correspondence. Eugene got a letter from home, telling him that all their horses had been taken, (presumably by the Russian army) except for one old mare. Maria also wrote to say she was going to come to try and find him. Poor lass! Let us hope that caution prevented her from trying to carry out her plan. As soon as the thaw set in the prisoners were sent to the far North by boat. Those two letters were the last Eugene ever heard from his family or friends at home. When they arrived at their destination, not too far from the Arctic Circle, they had to dig holes in the ground in which to live until they had built barracks. They were then to build the Pechora railway to open up the region to get at the oil and mineral wealth there. Conditions for the guards were probably not much better than for the prisoners, who were soon suffering from malnutrition in one form or another. The logistics of getting supplies to so many men must have been unimaginably difficult in those conditions. A few talked of trying to escape, but that would have meant almost certain death. There was nowhere to escape to, unless with the greatest of luck the escapees came across a group of Laplanders. These people were occasionally seen in the distance driving reindeer sleighs across the snow. One winter day Eugene tore his glove. He lost the tip of his index finger with frostbite. It rather spoiled his ability to play a guitar. When he complained that the pain was keeping him awake he was told that in that case he could keep the fires going through the night. Thousands died. Many more would have done if Hitler had not sent his armies to attack Russia in June 1941. After a great deal of prodding by Churchill, after Sikorski had been to see him, Stalin agreed that it was in his best interests to release the Polish prisoners to fight against the Germans. At first it was suggested that the Poles would fight alongside the Russians. Fortunately for all concerned this was decided against, as many Poles hated the Communists as much or even more than they hated the Germans. It was decided to form a Polish Army Corps right out of Russia. So the prisoners were sent by rail to the far South, travelling to the East of the Caspian Sea all the way down to Tashkent. Perhaps it was thought that, as the Germans were advancing so fast, they would be cut off if they were sent on the line running to the west of the Caspian sea. Travelling on through Tashkent they finally arrived in what was then Persia (now Iran). Here they were formed into units and sent to fight in North Africa. Eugene was a Bren Gun carrier driver for part of this time. They spent enough time in Egypt for him to visit the pyramids and other tourist attractions! Having driven the Germans out of Africa, the Polish soldiers were embarked for Italy. The troopship Eugene was on broke down in the middle of the Mediterranean. Until the engines were repaired they were a sitting duck, all alone whilst the convoy steamed on. Perhaps there were no U-boats or other German ships or planes available to attack them, but they were very relieved when they got going again.

As the allies moved up Italy, pushing the Germans out, Italian men would appear, waving rusty old rifles "We are Partisans!" they would claim. Eugene noticed that they never appeared until the last German had definitely gone.

Eugene's last war experience was in Monte Cassino. He took part in the final, successful push to the top, although he never reached it.

Before setting off each man was given a good swig of vodka. First to set off were soldiers with metal detectors to clear the mines. Eugene was in the next batch to go. They were ordered to ignore any of the mine clearers who had trodden on mines, lying wounded, often with their legs blown off.

Further up the mountain Eugene and his companions came up to a wall. As they suspected, Germans were hidden behind it. When grenades came flying over, he was crouching behind a rock. The grenade went off near enough for the explosion to perforate his ear drum, but otherwise he was unharmed. He chucked a grenade back over the wall, and that stopped any further trouble. They pressed on. Whether they got further ahead than allied artillery thought they were, or where the shrapnel came from, Eugene never knew, but a large piece hit his helmet, and bent the rim back to cut his neck. He spent a month in hospital and that was the end of fighting for him. He spent the rest of the time before coming to England in Italy learning a smattering of Italian. However, when he spoke it, I noticed that he was generally answered in English!

Eugene in Cambridge when he first came to England

CHAPTER 4
On the Move

We lived in Eugene's house in the middle of Cambridge for eighteen months after we got married until we could find somewhere with a bit of land. There was a strip of soil in our back yard in which I planted my 'can't-be-without-it' beet spinach. Our neighbours had put a trellis on top of the dividing wall. Nothing was growing on it, so I asked if she would mind if I planted runner beans to climb up it. She said she had never seen runners growing before, and never realised what pretty flowers they had. We agreed that we would each pick whichever beans grew on each side of the trellis. The wretched things all hung down on her side.

They were a lovely family; husband and wife and four boys, varying from fifteen to six years old. I didn't see much of the oldest one, but the other three often came round. They were beautifully brought up. If they went to play at a neighbour's house, they would go running round with their slippers in their hands. It did have its drawback. My housekeeping was criticised.

'Mummy dusts under there,' I was told.

I couldn't understand why the lads were so keen on my spinach. I was forever cooking it for them. One liked sugar on his. It was some time before I realised they had been reading *Popeye the Sailor Man*, who got his muscles from eating spinach.

Although the house was conveniently in the centre of Cambridge, we wanted to move for two main reasons. My mother had sold her house on the understanding that she could retain part of it at a peppercorn rent for her lifetime. She had offered us any furniture we would like and disposed of the rest. It was Victorian and Edwardian furniture which we both like, and I still do. We had it in store and had to find a house with large enough rooms to accommodate it. We also wished to have some land to start up some form of enterprise, as yet unknown. We started by cycling around Cambridge at every opportunity – south of Cambridge is more picturesque, and has a few bumps which could pass as hills for want of anything better. However, the soil to the north is of much better quality for small scale production. We knew we could never rake up sufficient funds to go in for 'proper' farming.

One estate agent gave us the keys to a bungalow with several acres attached. The bungalow was in a poor state of repair, and unsupervised viewing had made it even worse. On poking about on the land, we discovered large slabs of concrete which would have taken a lot of effort to remove. It turned out that the previous owner had had numerous cages and pens for animals. We turned the place down.

The next holding we viewed was somewhat larger. It was being run as a pig farm, and was immaculate. The owner was selling due to poor health. He had probably worked himself into the ground. We made him an offer which he refused. As it had a public footpath running slap through the middle of the land, it was perhaps as well we didn't get it.

Finally we found a suitable house in Histon, with one acre of land. That would do for a start, as we had yet to work out exactly what we were going to produce. The owners were an elderly couple, who had bought it when they retired eight years before. They had originally intended to breed fancy poultry to show. They had had a stab at it without much success, so had turned over to outdoor flower production in a mild sort of way. They had both lived in the village all their lives and had grown up in this area of many small, often part-time growers. The house had been built in 1923. The first owners were elderly, and were not used to having cooking facilities in the house. This was done in a separate building, generally known as the wash-house. Neither had it a bathroom. Originally it had had two good-sized bedrooms and a very small one in the front and another fair-sized one at the back. This one had been turned into a bathroom. The cold water tank sat on top of the airing cupboard. It was very rusty, but lasted all the time we were there by dint of being undisturbed.

There was an electrical socket in the bathroom, so I plugged in the spin dryer there until we had the re-wiring done. No way was the electrician going to put a socket in the bathroom. I pointed out that I would have to have an arm ten foot long to reach it from the bath or wash basin. He was adamant, no socket. He put one just outside the door where I could catch my foot in the flex and fall down the stairs. Whichever owner put the bath in still couldn't accept having a toilet in the house. We had had enough of going out in the cold. Luckily for us, in that respect, a developer was building two houses on land he had persuaded the previous owners to sell to him. He was building them on the side adjacent to our bathroom. The planning office put a small red line on the plans, enabling us to connect our sewage system to that of the new houses and therefore have a toilet put in the bathroom.

The developer was one of those people who are so sharp they cut themselves. The builder told us, 'I won't charge you very much, I'll put most of it on his bill.'

It was spring 1960 when we moved to our new premises. The

garden was so overgrown that we decided to more or less ignore it for that season and concentrate on the house. The previous owner could make a beautiful job of a few square yards of the garden, but while he did that the rest went into a wilderness.

The house did not seem to have had much done to it since it had been built nearly forty years before. Adding to the problems, the mortar was of poor quality and we discovered that the type of bricks used became porous after a time. The previous occupants had been advised that they would have to re-plaster several walls; a waste of time and money while the walls leaked every time it rained. Eugene repointed the walls on the weather sides and then we painted on a silicon-based liquid that made the rain run off like water off a duck's back. Having stopped the rain coming in, Eugene set to work on re-plastering. He had had plenty of practice in our last home, nearly driving me mad going round tapping the walls and pulling dusty old plaster off every time I thought I had at last got things looking a bit respectable.

Trying to open the casement windows was not exactly taking your life in your hands, but to risk losing them. Ropes that were not already broken did so as soon as the windows were moved. A friend of Eugene's replaced the rotten ropes with good quality new ones. Then I set to work on painting. Americans had rented some of the rooms. They were terrified of fresh air, and taped all around the windows. It had been there so long that it was impossible to pull off, and I had to scrape it a bit at a time. Noticing a damp patch on the chimney breast, I put my hand up the chimney and pulled down piles of chewed sacking, complete with silverfish. The painting kept me quiet for a long time. (There were twenty-two panes of glass in the windows just in our bedroom.)

Having got the house in reasonable order, we turned our attention to the land. Scything and chopping through the wilderness, we found all sorts of odds and ends. All too much for one family, but not enough to be any use commercially. There was a small orchard, consisting of five Laxton Superb eating apples and one large old Bramley covered in bristles, as it had once been carefully pruned and then neglected. There were two or three Conference pear trees, and various plums. Right at the bottom of the garden was a row of old greengage trees, with only one or two branches left on each one. From these we got our first lesson in the attitude of retailers. These greengages had a most wonderful flavour when ripe. We found that we got half the price when they were nicely ripe, but in no way overripe, than we did if we sold them when they were hard and green, and would have no flavour even when they softened up. The retailer could keep them much longer that way, but I think it was one of the ways that ruined the plum market.

During his scything operations, Eugene stumbled over a row of raspberries and also, festooned with weeds, were the twiggy remains of a row of redcurrant bushes. These I learned to prune by studying how a knowledgeable neighbour did his. For some reason, Eugene found the way I stood back to try to work out how to tackle each bush very amusing. I think he was waiting for me to actually stand on my head to get the best view. I got to greatly like these bushes. After a year or two of removing the weak branches and pruning back the new side shoots on the strongest older branches, the berries they produced were like jewels. Very relaxing to pick by sitting on a pouffe, especially as they were ready just after the hectic period of strawberry picking.

There were a few rows of daffodils which we dug up and replanted in the orchard. Just a waste of space in the open ground. Not enough to be worth sending away, and other areas had earlier daffs, to get better prices.

Our orchard

We grew a few potatoes that first season and stored them in one of the sheds, covering them with 'hay' from the grass Eugene had scythed off. Someone had given my mother a kitten. She brought it to us, saying she couldn't keep it as people complained about it digging in their gardens. He took to sleeping on the top of the potatoes. We discovered that rats, who had probably benefited from chicken food in the past, had got into the shed and attacked the potatoes.

Eugene said, 'They are bouncing the cat up and down as they operate under him.'

We dug deep trenches round all the sheds, nailed wire netting well up the sides of the sheds, and bedded it. We managed to stop them, but not before a neighbour complained, '*your* rats are running about and playing in our garden.' Our rats! Did she think we kept them as pets?

We hadn't decided what we were going to do, but whatever it was, an acre of garden would not be enough. So we started to make enquiries. Not far down the road was a man with several glasshouses. He might know where there might be an acre or two near at hand. He did. There was a man who lived in Garden Walk, who he thought was thinking of selling some of his land.

'Oh, I don't know his name,' he told us, 'but he stutters. Anyone will tell you who he is.'

So an evening or two later we set off. A little man was walking towards us down Garden Walk. Eugene explained that we were interested in buying a bit more land and were looking for a man whose name we didn't know.

'He can't talk properly,' added Eugene helpfully.

'I, I, have ger, ger, got some le, l, land for sale,' said the little man.

I wasn't sure whether to try to sink into the ground or hit Eugene over the head, but the little man didn't seem a bit put out. Once upon a time he and his father had kept a few cows, but these had gone long ago. John was now getting on a bit and had recently been ill. His few acres had got too much for him, and he was probably a bit short of cash, as it didn't look as if he had had much to sell for some time. John sold us three-and-a-half acres directly behind our land, but separated from ours by a couple of orchards and a bit of land used for flowers and soft fruit. We reached it by going up the road a couple of hundred yards and then down a track.

The soils in that area were very mixed, from greensand to heavy clay. On the soil map ours appeared as 'Raised River Terrace', presumably left from the last Ice Age. Reasonably fertile and easily worked, one of our neighbours referred to it as 'dry overhead' land, although not very far down was heavy clay – up from which popped a profusion of Mare's Tail.

The top soil being quite light, our neighbour said, 'Don't put your coat down on it, it will eat it', meaning it was hungry soil. It was also alkaline with a pH of 7.9. No lime needed. So what were we going to do with our little empire? We toyed with all sorts of ideas, even considering poultry, which I felt I might just put up with if they were ours. I would have liked to have specialised in calf-rearing for dairy farmers, taking the calves off them at a week old, and returning them when reared. Many cowmen were not enamoured with having to bother with calves, and I had plenty of experience. If we had had the buildings, I would have tried to get local dairy farmers interested. Chivers had red and white Friesians and Jerseys. There was a very large herd at West Wratting and plenty of other dairy herds about at the time. Then came the time of 'butter mountains' and dairy farmers were offered a golden handshake in the 1980's to quit milk production. Both the Chivers and West Wratting herds went.

A little while after this, the gardens at West Wratting were open. We went to see them. I wandered off to the deserted dairy buildings. It was sad to see. The farm workers had discarded their white jackets after the final milking and there was still a tin of udder salve left open. Outside the house I saw an elderly lady who appeared to be giving information to visitors, so I went to have a word with her. It turned out to be Lady D'Abo. She told me that the cattle had been her life's work. When she had got married there had only been a few nondescript beasts, with an elderly stockman in charge. She had built it up over the years. Unfortunately when her husband died, the property was left in trust. Money being the trust managers' priority, they were only too pleased to take up the Government's offer. Poor Lady D'Abo was heartbroken. She said how she would look out into the park to see the cattle grazing, and now all the great trees had wheat growing all round them.

One of our more way-out ideas was to consider producing Sauerkraut (pickled cabbage). Eugene knew how to do it, as his family had made it. So we purchased a small wooden cask and set to work. Where he came from they knew they would get hot summers and cold winters – ideal for the pickling process in the summer and to keep it well during the cold weather. If we had had a hot summer when we tried it, it might have worked, but the weather turned cold and wet, and our shredded cabbage just went mouldy. To make Sauerkraut in the UK it would be necessary to have a controlled environment, and that would be far too expensive.

In the end we decided to do what was staring us in the face. Whether the set-up was unique to the villages just north of Cambridge, I don't know, but I had never come across it before. Many people had small areas of land, from big gardens to a few acres. On this they grew mainly soft fruit and flowers, often on a part-time basis. There were agents in the villages who would go round with their lorries, collect the produce and take it to their yards. Here lorries from all over the country would come, from London, Birmingham, Manchester, Bradford and probably more. You chose where, and to which salesman you wanted to send it. Some things did better in certain towns. For instance, peonies as cut flowers did best in Manchester. Once established, we found Birmingham was our best market, and we kept to the same salesman who got to know our produce, and to know it was well packed. The exception was for pumpkins. We sent them all the way to Bradford.

The reason for this set-up was historical. For centuries Cottenham had been renowned for its cheese. Up to a thousand head of cattle would go out onto the common pastureland each day, returning in the evening where each small group would know where it belonged. The reason this continued into the nineteenth century was because early enclosures of the sixteenth century were successfully resisted by the inhabitants of Cottenham. However, in the nineteenth century the common land was enclosed. The final blow to cheese production was in the mid-1800s when the herds were devastated by cattle plague (Rinderpest). After this the small areas of land they still had available were put to intensive use, for example for the growing of cut flowers and soft fruit, the latter being encouraged after the Chivers jam factory was set up.

Histon and Impington were rather different. A few large landowners, and sheep predominating rather than cattle. The proximity to Cambridge led to the development of market gardening in the early nineteenth century. Then of course in 1873, Stephen Chivers founded the jam factory, which had an impact on all the surrounding areas with the demand for soft and top fruit.

Neither Eugene nor I knew anything about growing flowers or soft fruit. I had grown some vegetables on a domestic scale. Eugene's family had just planted a new orchard when he was called up. They also grew tobacco. Eugene said the tobacco in bought cigarettes was not strong enough, so he tried growing a bit for himself. He soon decided it wasn't worth the bother.

We set about finding what was hiding amongst the jungle in the garden. Anything we thought might be useful was cleared round or moved to a fresh bit of ground. As well as raspberries and redcurrants, there was a row of blackcurrants. As well as the daffodils we put under the fruit trees, we found Wirral Supreme, a variety of Chrysanthemum Maximum, and an unknown variety of scabious, a few spindly Spanish irises, and other odds and ends.

As I had my job at the University, we could take our time getting sorted out and deciding what to grow. Without this income we would not have been able to get established.

CHAPTER 5
Finding Out What to Do

Many of the local growers just had big gardens and would only be picking a crop for a few weeks each year. Most of the full-time growing was based on orchards, often under-planted with pyrethrums which were a favourite flower in the locality. We were aiming to earn our income from our holding, and needed to be harvesting something for as many months of the year as possible.

We took to 'spying' to get ideas of various flowers, and to note when they were picked. I had heard of a book we thought would be very useful to us – *The Flower Grower's Handbook* by Roy Genders. I was told it was out of print. I tried everywhere – no luck. Having given up, months later I was looking for something else and spotted a forgotten copy on a bookseller's shelf. I was thrilled. It proved to be one of the best purchases I have ever made. It showed the correct method to pack cut flowers. The elderly couple we had bought the house from had been very helpful in showing us how they packed them, with rolled-up newspaper for 'pillows' to protect the heads. Purchasing proper packing paper and following professional methods improved our returns considerably. We also learnt the importance of having a named variety. Scabious grew very well in the limey soil, in fact that book recommended putting lime in the hole when planting. With our high pH, that was not necessary. There were some scabious on the holding when we got it, but variety unknown. As

Roy Genders called it his 'bread and butter' flower because it had such a long flowering period, from July until well into autumn, we decided to get some Clive Greaves – the recommended variety. The plants were expensive, so we just bought a few and kept splitting them until we had enough to make up a few boxes. They made about double the amount the un-named variety had. Why they were such a popular cut flower, I was never sure, as they didn't have a very long vase life.

Why we decided to grow gladioli, I'm not sure. It might just have been that I remembered getting my mother a bunch of salmon pink gladioli and powder blue scabious and thought how lovely they were. Anyhow, we planted corms of two varieties, bright pink General Eisenhower and delicate salmon pink Picardy. We built up numbers by planting on the cormlets. They were a real pain, having to be carefully weeded by hand. We had built them up to quite a good number when we were hit by one of the coldest winters for decades; winter 1962/3. We had no central heating. Although we tried all ways to keep the corms from freezing, we lost the lot. In a way it was no bad thing. They were too big to pack in standard flower boxes. We took most of them to the produce market in Cambridge but they never made much. I remembered my mother telling me that her relatives used to keep roses to sell at Christmas by some cunning trick. I wondered how we might do the same with the glads. One of our customers had a freezer, so we got them to pop a bunch in there. It didn't work. When lifted out, they didn't wait to thaw before falling into bits.

I'll never forget that winter. It wasn't too bad for me as I was still at work, and somehow the offices kept quite warm. As the electricity was off more than it was on, I don't know how that was done. I walked to work and back. It was the best way to keep warm, and in any case buses were abandoned at the sides of the road as the diesel froze. Eugene did the best he could by knocking down and sawing up woodworm-riddled sheds and burning them. Approaching the house one evening, I passed a muffled-up figure.

I said, 'Good evening.'

Very politely the 'stranger' returned my greeting. I had gone yards up the road before realising it was Eugene, who had come to meet me. Every evening before we went to bed, we would walk round the block as fast as we could go, leaving an electric fire on in our bedroom if there wasn't a power cut. On arriving home we would dive into bed, leaving just our noses uncovered.

We were very sorry for the elderly couple who had only moved into the new bungalow next door a few months before. It was all electric. I don't know how they managed to survive. We had gas for cooking, which didn't get cut off. Every evening I had to remember to fill a kettle with water. The cold water pipe was flush up against the outside wall, and couldn't be lagged. In the morning I boiled the kettle, and put hot rags on the pipe. Fortunately it worked. If it hadn't, we would have been really stuck. Having got water, I would then take them a pot of tea, have some breakfast, head for work and leave them all to cope. The neighbour next to them wasn't much better off. He had central heating but, as it depended on an electrical pump, it wasn't much use. That was one of the main reasons we didn't get central heating put in. We put in solid fuel room heaters which were expensive to run and made a lot of dust, but were very efficient.

The River Cam was frozen solid. People were playing ice hockey on it. I walked on the ice under all the bridges at the back of the colleges. It was dreadful for the poor birds. One morning I passed a hedge with a few remaining berries on it. It was covered with fieldfares, so desperate they took no notice of me. Close up it was possible to see how beautiful they were, with their blue-grey backs and speckled chests. It was a very sad sight.

As the land either side of our house had been sold, we had no means of getting a tractor into the garden. The drive led straight to the garage, next to our neighbour's garden on the right hand side. There would have been room on the left hand side if a large cherry tree had not been smack in the way. It was slowly dying when we got there. Whether the die-back from gum disease was the reason branches had been cut off, or cutting them off had been the cause of the trouble, we didn't know. 'Thinking' it was dying, the tree was covered with fruit every year. Unfortunately we got very few. The birds would insist on stripping it before the cherries were ripe. We tried everything. Nothing placed in the tree frightened them. I even tried to get next door's cat to sit up there, but she had as much idea of climbing as a tortoise. I heard her yelling, 'Help, help!' one day, to find her clinging to a pile of rather wobbly cardboard boxes all of seven feet off the ground.

The only times we reversed the van round under the cherry tree, was in the autumn to put potatoes and pumpkins in to store in one of the sheds. We didn't realise that it was sinking sideways further each year. I got firmly stuck under a large branch one day and we had to let the tyres down to get out.

Although the garden was only an acre, we needed something to cultivate it with. Rotovating alone is not very satisfactory. It tends to work to the same depth all the time, making a hard pan; fine to get rid of annual weeds or if you want a fine tilth, but not so good in autumn, when it would cap over by the spring. We found a two-wheeler called an Autoculto. The dealer had been established for many years, so we felt any problems could be dealt with. It was our bad luck that the son took over the business, got over-ambitious and went bankrupt.

That Autoculto was trouble. It had a beautiful, single-furrow plough which made an excellent job for a short while. We should have known it wasn't strong enough for the job, as it had a chain drive. The chain kept stretching. To shorten it, you moved the gearbox housing back a bit. Then you couldn't get the wretched thing in gear or, worse still, out of it. We had made a temporary place to propagate seeds from old window frames until we built a proper glasshouse. We then used this covered area to house the Autoculto. I heard Eugene – well, it was a good job I couldn't hear what he said. He had been unable to stop the machine, and it had gone straight through the glass at the back. The man who was doing our machinery repairs by that time, recommended driving it into a brick wall to stop it!

The Autoculto also had a rotovator. To use this the wheels had to be changed from large rim ones to smaller pneumatics. It was a heavy and tedious job. So we invested in a Howard Rotovator. It was a brilliant machine. Eugene wouldn't allow me to use it until his rheumatism made stumbling behind it too difficult. He then stood at the ends of the rows of plants waiting for me to smash into them. It was actually very easy to manage, easier than a lighter machine would have been as it did the job itself if handled properly.

We got a contractor to cultivate the field. He ploughed it and then put cultivators over it, as the Howard couldn't cope with the ridges; it plunged and tossed about so much that the blades were in the air more than in the soil.

We tried all kinds of crops for the first few years before settling into a suitable cropping pattern. The first plants to be ready to harvest were the pyrethrums – 'pys' in play, followed by Dutch Irises in late May-June. Then strawberries and other soft fruit. In August most other growers were picking plums. We didn't have any worth mentioning, so went for runner beans. August, September we picked marrows; after a few years courgettes came into fashion, so we changed over to those. September to Christmas, depending on the frost, we were cutting cauliflowers. Pumpkins were cut and stored as soon as they were ripe, before they got frosted.

From July until late in the autumn we had scabious. In autumn there were bunching chrysanthemums. We always hoped they would peak for the Jewish New Year, as the price then shot up.

We also grew two or three hundredweight of garlic. Any spare land was planted with potatoes. Annual/biennial flower crops were soon discontinued. We tried Sweet Williams, cornflowers, stocks, larkspur and statice. The seed was expensive, weeding and thinning seedlings was very time consuming and they made very little money for the work involved. Perennials could be divided *ad infinitum* once you had got your stock established. Being bigger plants they were also much easier to keep weed-free.

As well as giving up the annuals, we also gave up the Wirral Supremes after a few years. They were like a double Ox-eye Daisy. To make any money they had to be dyed. After bunching, their heads were dipped in a fixative, then into special flower dye. Laddie Pink was a favoured colour, but much more expensive than the other dyes, so we used red or yellow. Some people dyed them blue, or even green, but that looked very odd to me. The bunches were then hung on nails all around the shed to dry. My mother came to visit, and was very intrigued by the dyeing. She said, 'No wonder the florist's girl grinned when I said, "I can't grow flowers that colour."'

One of the reasons we stopped growing them was that they had to be picked when we were busy with the more lucrative soft fruit.

Also, if there was a heavy summer storm, they would be flattened, and would only pick up the heads and a short bit of stalk, so were impossible to bunch.

A plant that was in the garden when we took over, and which we probably ought to have kept, was the Sea Lavender Latifolia. It looked to us as if it would be difficult to pack, and did not seem very attractive. The carrier who took produce to the auction market in Cambridge hated it. However secure he thought he had made it, it would wriggle free and go bouncing down the road like Tumbleweed. It was only a good many years later when I saw that the agent we were then using had sheds and a field full of it, that I decided we had made a mistake.

CHAPTER 6
Flowers

Neither of us knew anything about growing cut flowers on a commercial scale, so it was fortunate that we had about five years to learn the ropes and build up our stocks while I was still employed by the University.

After a few years we developed a routine. As soon as the soil was dry and warm enough in the spring, we would renew our stock of Pyrethrums by splitting up the old plants. We had two varieties – Kelway Glory, which were bright red and the earlier, followed by Eileen May Robinson, a lovely China pink. The pys were ready to cut from early May. Each kind of flower had to be harvested at the right stage of opening. Pys needed to be almost fully open. Scabious could be cut in the half-open stage, and before the 'pin cushion' in the middle had opened. Irises and gladioli had to be picked as soon as they showed a bit of colour in the bud. We didn't grow peonies, but our neighbours had about half an acre of Sarah Bernhardt, a pinky cream with a good scent. These had to be cut when the bud was just getting soft. Eschscholzia (or Californian) Poppies were no longer grown, as far as we knew, but we were told that they would arrive at market in bud. The salesman would take a bunch, gently bang it on his leg, and the whole bunch would fly open in glorious technicolour.

When we first started growing pys, we thought someone was playing games and cutting them before we could. We discovered it was hares. They loved them. Perhaps they were the hares' spring cure for worms or other parasites. They are, or were, grown in other countries to make into insecticide. To stop the hares and rabbits from eating our profits, we put chicken wire all around the field. The hares came across a bridge over a wide ditch to gain access. One year we ran out of wire netting. We only needed a few yards at the far end of the field.

'They won't get all the way round to find that gap,' said Eugene confidently.

I agreed, 'No, of course they won't. We can get some more before the rabbits become a nuisance.' It took the hares about two days to find the gap. That was not all. Our dog chased one one day. When it reached the wire it just climbed over.

'It's using it for a ladder,' said my husband, his eyes popping out of his head in disbelief.

Having found they could climb the wire, the mother hares must have decided it would make a secure nursery. It seemed that they would climb over, have a nibble of pys, and feed any leverets they had hidden. The dog would often find these beautiful little creatures. As they didn't run away, he would prod them with his nose. He would probably have eaten them, but when I heard one squeal I had time to grab the dog and tie him up.

By the time I was due to finish working at the University we had built up a good area of pys. That was when near-disaster struck. I came home to find Eugene in bed complaining of chest pains. As his mother had died when only forty-six of bronchial asthma, and a sister with double pneumonia at just twenty-one years of age, I sent for the doctor straight away. He had a temperature of 104F. Pneumonia, the doctor said. I knew what he had been up to. My mother had drilled into me the danger of getting chilled after sweating from exertion, or heat.

'Always put on a cardigan,' she said.

Eugene had been hoeing the emerging irises on a hot May afternoon. The neighbours were taking tea in their garden, and invited him to join them. This he did, and that was when he must have got chilled. The doctor was concerned that his temperature remained very high. I had to give him pills every four hours, day and night. I was so tired that I decided that I would have to leave the pys, although we now depended on the holding for our living. Times like these are when you find out who your real friends are. On my way down to the field when Eugene was first ill, I passed George Hacker working on his land. He asked where Eugene was, and I told him Eugene was in bed with pneumonia. On the following Sunday afternoon, I saw a car come into our drive. My heart sank; I could not cope with visitors. It was George.

'My daughter has come over, and we will go down and give you a start on the pys.'

They were experts, having been cultivating pys for years, and romped through the lot in a little over two hours. I was then able to keep up with the rest as they opened.

Thankfully Eugene recovered, but he was too anxious to get back to work, which didn't help his health for the future.

As soon as, or even before, the pys had finished, the irises would start popping out. We had a few early Wedgewoods that were there when we came. They were pale blue, and didn't seem very popular; so we didn't get any more of them. Unlike most of our other flowers, we couldn't buy just a few irises and split them up. We splashed out quite a considerable sum to plant up a third of our acre; a dark blue variety called Imperator, and a bright yellow called Golden Harvest. Irises have to be picked as soon as the buds show a bit of colour, and packed before they open. We had no-one to instruct us, so developed our own systems, referring to the flower growers' book where possible. I always thought how strange it was that the price you got seemed to depend more on the length of stem. What is the first thing you do when you go to put a bunch of flowers in a vase? Usually cut at least a foot off the stems. Pys were nearly all the same height, so we bunched them – a dozen to a bunch – as we picked them. Irises varied in height. Our usual method was for Eugene to cut them and bring them in to me to bunch. I would separate them into three lengths in piles, then make bunches of six by taking two from each pile. Quite often there were short ones left over, and these we used to take to Cambridge auction market, or put them out the front in a bucket of water.

Putting anything out for people to help themselves was always a risk, so we only did it with a few leftover flowers that hadn't got another home to go to. Sometimes you got the money left, and sometimes you didn't. One enterprising youth took to cycling up and down helping himself to any cash left by honest folk. I learnt an interesting lesson in not judging people by appearances. George Hacker was a very good, able grower, often propagating unusual and difficult plants. Once he had several of these to sell; I can't remember exactly what they were. He told his wife he would just put out three or four of them at a time. As he came in, having put out the first batch, he saw a big car show up, and a smartly dressed lady step out. He said he didn't want to disturb her and look 'pushy', so he waited until the car drove off. All the plants had gone but there was no money left for them.

One summer evening I had put out a few leftovers. I saw that there were only a couple of bunches left as I passed them to take the dog out for a walk. On the way back, when I was several hundred yards up the road, I saw that a tatty old lorry had stopped, and a roughly dressed man was standing near the flowers. As I got closer, I saw his wife and several kids were squeezed into the front seat. They looked like a family of gypsies.

'Oh well,' I thought. 'I haven't lost much.' I was sure that they would have pinched them. Why was he taking such a long time? I wondered what other mischief he was up to.

The lorry finally drove off. I felt very ashamed for judging him just because he looked rough. The reason he had taken so long was that the family had laboriously counted out the money with all the loose change they had between them.

Our neighbour, George Hacker, was discussing returns on cut flowers with us one day. He said, 'It is on a long sheet of paper, and the bit you get is right at the bottom. Very often it will drop off altogether.'

The gross price would appear at the top, followed by deductions, such as hire of boxes, transport and commission.

One Whitsun, George's prediction came true. It had been unusually cold and dull. The irises stayed firmly shut. On the Friday afternoon, too late to send any more blooms until the following Tuesday, out came the sun. Determined to make up for poor performance, it blazed forth, the whole weekend being a real heatwave. Lovely for most of the population heading off to watch the waves swishing in and out, but not for us. The irises woke up and started to open. We only just managed to keep up. Then what to do with them? Put in water they would open up and be impossible to pack. We laid them out on the concrete floor, but were afraid to make it damp as they would go mouldy. A fan would have helped, but as we didn't have one we hung up wet sheets to shade the blooms. The first day it was possible to send the irises off was on the Tuesday afternoon after Whitsun. Of course nobody would want them then. Before the holiday they would have made a useful little present to take someone. We packed thirty-four cases with thirty-six bunches in each, six blooms to a bunch. That is 1224 bunches, six blooms in a bunch, equals 7344 blooms. You would expect to get a pound or two from that, wouldn't you? I don't remember what we got per case gross, but the sum total we got for the whole lot after deductions was ten shillings (50p)! I rang the salesman. He said he had hundreds, no thousands of cases to get rid of. 'I did manage to sell yours and another grower's from the local consignments.' Most of the growers had to pay transport for no sale. It seemed that it had been dull and cold everywhere up until Whitsun. West Country, Channel Isles, the lot. Then the sun had come blazing out everywhere. We never had quite such a disaster again, but it showed the need to grow a wide range of produce.

I have already said that we discarded annual flowers after a few years. Wirral Supreme and gladioli after a year or two. We tried a small area of Alstromeria – Ligtu Hybrids hoping they might flower after the soft fruit finished, but they came smack in the middle of the strawberry season. They were also a puzzle to pack as they came in such a variety of lengths. Sometimes they made a good price, and sometimes next to nothing, so we didn't expand the area we had planted. In the end we settled for pys, irises, bunching chrysanthemums, the very useful Clive Greaves Scabious, which went on flowering for several months into the autumn.

Scabious

CHAPTER 7
Soft Fruit

When we first took over the one acre garden, it was totally overgrown. Gradually we unearthed a wide variety of plants, all grown for sale, but in tiny amounts. A row of raspberries was festooned with weeds, and when we freed them from this encumbrance they proved to be such poor, straggly creatures, yielding little dried-up fruit that even we, with our inexperience, realised they were useless. We dug them up. A few raspberries for local sale might be useful, so we put in a couple of rows of Glen Cova. We were quite right not to go overboard on raspberries. The East Anglian climate is not the best for them. They also take much longer to pick than strawberries. There was a row of blackcurrants and a short row of redcurrants. We kept the former basically because they were there. The ones we didn't sell, I made into jam – one of the easiest to set and best. The redcurrants we kept for a different reason. There were only about twenty redcurrant bushes when we took over the garden; hardly worth bothering with. We kept them mainly for one reason. I did use them to mix with raspberries to make jam, once having made redcurrant jelly which didn't set. Then once, having tried to make jelly which didn't set, I discovered it made a lovely drink, which from then on I used it for. Naturally I expected it to set each year in the bottles, but it didn't.

The main reason we kept the redcurrants was because they were such a joy. They were ready to pick as the strawberries finished. After the hurly-burly of the last four weeks, to sit under the bushes on a comfortable pouffe was wonderfully relaxing. Also they were so beautiful. Having pruned them into shape, the berries hung down in long strings of sparkling iridescent jewels.

Our main soft fruit crop was strawberries. We tried one or two different varieties before settling for Cambridge Favourite. It yielded well and had a very good flavour; perhaps not as good as Royal Sovereign, which had been developed at Water Perry, but Royal Sovereign suffered from the disease Red Core, so we avoided that. We only grew about half an acre, some in the garden and some down the field, but that was enough to cope with, with just a few pickers. One of our neighbours had about six acres, but they just picked a few of the early ones themselves for sale through the agent and the rest went to Chivers' factory. Every evening the grass verge would be buried in bikes belonging to an army of kids.

This six acre field of strawberries was never replanted with new plants. If it was a wet season they got a reasonable crop, otherwise they would get very little. It was part of quite a large county council farm, with the grandfather, father and grandson running it.

We found it paid to replace the strawberry plants every three to four years. It was recommended that you should not pick them during the first year, but as they were the earliest and big fat juicy fruits, temptation was usually too much. Then we let the runners grow into what was called a matted row.

We tried having one or two kids for picking, but they were pretty useless. They were too rough to pick anything to go into punnets. They liked to throw any mouldy ones at each other, and would get over-enthusiastic and chuck the whole lot all over the place. We stuck to a few local ladies. Most of them were members of a keep fit class.

Some were better pickers than others. One very conscientious lady, trying to make them look nicer in the punnet, would touch them. After an hour or so you could see every mark. Any destined for the factory would be 'coshed', which was the local term for hulling them.

One rather elderly picker said to me, 'I have put the biggest ones on the top of the punnets.'

Did they think nobody got to those underneath?

We wanted to get a reputation for good presentation, so I said to her, 'No, dear, if they are not good enough to go on the top, they are not good enough to go in the punnet.'

It was not a very bright thing to say. I should have added that the smaller ones should go in different punnets, however, I didn't. The next day I came through the gate just as one of the best pickers was leaving. She had a large bicycle basket full of strawberries.

'I thought these ones were not good enough to go in the punnets,' she said. Ah, well.

George Hacker recommended us to try to get a certain Mrs Smith to come to pick for us. She was a large lady in her sixties. She had lived in the village all her life. I mentioned going for a walk down Gun's Lane, which was a track believed to be part of the Roman road or even earlier, to Ely. She asked us if the old cottage was still there. It had been deserted when she was a little girl at the beginning of the twentieth century. It stood in what had been the old cottager's garden. By the time we went down there, only one or two stray bricks remained of the dwelling. The garden hadn't been touched for all that time. It was a fascinating wildlife haven of about an acre, full of birds and primroses in the spring. What had once been a hedge bordered the track. After about fifty or sixty years it had turned into a row of small trees twisted into grotesque shapes, which reminded me of the wild woods that frightened Snow White.

One late February afternoon, just as it was getting dusk, Eugene and I were walking past when migratory redwings decided to roost there for the night. There were thousands of them, wave after wave. The local birds were completely traumatised, and shot up into the air shrieking.

It was a few weeks later when we saw a pall of black smoke rising up from that direction. I went down to find smouldering devastation. It was a wicked thing to have done. There must have been birds nesting in there. Just to gain an odd-shaped acre of wet land. It was the time when farmers were being encouraged to tear up hedges and destroy old orchards. Having achieved the miracle of coming from a state of rationing in 1954 to overproduction in ten years, now farmers were told they had to go for productivity rather than simple production; in other words meaning that it had got to be efficient with regard to cost. This was the dawn of what I call the Canary Syndrome – cheap, cheap, cheap at any cost to the environment and the 'units of production', whether human or animal.

Mrs Smith was an exceptional person. She had been a school-teacher, but had always enjoyed working on the land. During the war she had taken any opportunity to help with tasks such as potato picking. Except for the soft fruit, we did nearly all the harvesting ourselves, apart from the pys which came in a rush when Eugene needed to get on with other jobs, such as rotovating. So Mrs Smith, who was an expert, helped me with them. The old way had been to tie the bunches with raffia, locally called bass. This was prepared and tied at the waist, ready to use. We used rubber bands which we bought by the pound. I made pouches to carry them in, handy to get at. Using a sharp, short-bladed knife, we put twelve flowers in a bunch. I fixed a small sheath below my knee, into which I dropped the knife while I put the bands on. Mrs Smith held hers between her teeth like a pirate boarding a ship.

However hot the weather, Mrs Smith wore enormous rubber boots. Her ability as a picker was second to none. One day we had a wedding order for fifty pounds of strawberries. I told Mrs Smith I had to do a delivery, but would be back in about an hour, when I would then give her a hand. I was no more than an hour, but when I got back she said that she had picked the fifty pounds and then gone back to half pound punnets, was that right? How many people would pick fifty pounds of strawberries in an hour? Twelve pounds is a reasonable amount.

Strawberries are best picked in cool conditions, such as early morning and evening. So we used to set off as soon as it was light every day, starting at soon after 4am, saying, 'We should beat old Mr Wilderspin this morning.' But we never did.

There he would be, nose almost touching the ground, on the path in front of us. He said he could no longer keep up with his son and grandson on the farm, so spent the whole year in the strawberry field. Most of the year he was weeding, putting the weeds in an old wooden wheelbarrow in which he sat at intervals for a rest.

We thought it must be possible to make picking strawberries less of a back-breaking job. After some thought, we designed 'picking trolleys'. At the front we put pram wheels, then a wooden tray, big enough to hold a strawberry tray and spare punnets, then a space which we called the search area, a seat on which you sat astride and bicycle wheels at the rear. This we placed over the rows and pushed with our feet either backwards or forwards, whichever you preferred. Most of our picking ladies held these trolleys in contempt, but I did see one of the plumper ones astride it and the bicycle wheels were taking on rather an odd angle, so I hastily went and took out employer's insurance. Eugene thought we perhaps made picking too comfortable, but as quite a few people showed an interest in our 'invention', we intended to produce a less Heath Robinson model for sale. However, great minds think alike. When we opened the *Commercial Grower* that Autumn, someone in Hampshire had produced something almost exactly the same and theirs even had a plastic cover over it!

Eugene and Barbus on a strawberry picking trolley

Most of our pickers wanted to work from nine o'clock onwards. This was fine for raspberries, which I discovered could only be picked if really dry. In those days punnets did not have to be weighed. One evening, when as far as I knew it was still quite dry, I decided the punnets needed a few more raspberries in each one; so I picked a few more. The next morning they had all gone mouldy, and I had to throw away all the ones I had picked in the evening. Some of

Eugene's friends would come and help in the evenings, especially one family consisting of the father, John, and five kids. I was still working in Cambridge when he brought them out the first time. They were very young and not easily controlled. Eugene said all five (the youngest three were triplets) erupted from the car and spread out in all directions, not only on our land, but neighbours' also, where they proceeded to pull up everything within reach. They had to be rounded up and locked in the car. However, a few years later they really became quite useful. The oldest lad liked counting and weighing. They were all very bright kids, except for one of the triplets. She was so different in all ways, including looks, that you wouldn't have known they were related. Eugene said he wondered how she would get on when she grew up. He needn't have worried. When we had finished picking one evening, we said they could have some fruit for themselves. The two bright ones grabbed empty punnets and ran off to pick some. The dull one? She helped herself to a full punnet!

When I first met Eugene, he and his friends spoke to each other in Ukrainian or Polish. He could understand Russian, but not speak it. He also spoke some Italian, although I noticed Italians often answered him in English.

He said that when he first arrived in England, he thought what a funny language it was. So it is. Unless you have grown up with it, it must be very confusing. You raise something up, then you raze it to the ground. You have mice in the houses, but never mouses in the hice. One day we saw some Chinese geese in a neighbour's garden.

'Look at the pretty gooses!' said Eugene.

'No, no!' I told him. 'The plural of goose is geese.'

'OK,' says he obligingly. 'Look at the pretty geeses.'

Then there are the different pronunciations for the –ough ending: dough, plough, rough, through, cough and possibly more. The story goes that in the days when there were fewer foreigners travelling in England, a Frenchman went into a chemist's shop to get some medicine. He had looked up the appropriate words in his dictionary.

'Could I have something,' he asked, 'for a cow on his box?'

Eastern Europeans do not use the 'ph' and 'th' sounds. Once I thought Eugene said, 'I want to go to Nottingham today.' I wondered why he should want to go to Nottingham. What he had actually said was, 'I want to go to Nutting and Thoday.'

There were seed merchants at Westwick. We were walking down to the field when a bird with a long tail rose up just in front of us.

'Look at that peasant,' says Eugene.

'No, dear,' says I. 'That's a pheasant, we're the peasants.'

I rather hoped he was not aware of what the snooty English infer when they call someone a peasant!

Old cultivator found deserted down Gun's Lane

CHAPTER 8
Finding a Way to Sell Our Produce

The most convenient way to sell produce was through the agents who sent goods to various markets in lorries, which went to salesmen in towns such as London, Birmingham, Manchester and even Bradford. You just had to pack the goods. For flowers, even the wooden boxes were supplied for the first few years we were operating. You could either deliver them to the agent's yard, or he would collect them. This method we continued to use for nearly all the flowers, generally sending them to a salesman in Birmingham. If we had grown peonies they did best in Manchester, we were told. We tried London once or twice, but Birmingham seemed much better. I approached several retailers at first. One said he got all his flowers from Spitalfields. No doubt they had gone up there and come back again. One wanted a few on a 'sale or return' basis. He simply put them in a bucket of water and doubled the price. I did find a very good florist near Fen Causeway, conveniently on my route to Cambridge Auction Market. We offered to plant specially for him, but he said the public were so fickle that he never knew what they wanted. Some of them would also have flowers for a special occasion, such as weddings and funerals, for which it seemed they had no intention of paying. Bad debts were a constant worry for him.

We had an odd corner in the field, which one year we planted up with Globe Artichokes from seed. We knew that these probably wouldn't make very good edible heads, so we did it just to try them out. Big tall plants led some of our neighbours to enquire what we were growing.

'Shh!' I said. 'Marijuana!'

I expected an earnest policeman to appear at any moment.

We tried a few of the globes, but they were not very fleshy, so we left them to open. They were like huge thistle flowers, the local bees thought they were in paradise. Thinking they might make an interesting subject for flower arrangers, I asked our florist friend if he would like to have some. He put them in his window over the weekend and when I went past on the Monday morning, I was really ashamed to see they had all gone mouldy, although I had been careful to pick them when, as far as I knew, they were completely dry. I felt very ashamed.

Although sending nearly all the flowers through the agent was perfectly satisfactory, it was a different matter with soft fruit. Flowers went to a salesman who just got commission, so he got the best price he could. However the fruit and vegetables went to a wholesaler. We kept happily sending strawberries for the whole of our first season. Returns, which all came by post in those days, arrived very quickly for a few days, and then dried up. In our innocence, we thought it was just because the wholesaler was very busy. When we received our payment at the end of the strawberry season, we discovered that after the first ten days we only made enough to cover the pickers' wages. Something obviously had to be done about this. We should look around for other outlets. Retailers were generally useless, they only wanted a few pounds at a time. We started sending to Cambridge Auction Market and got a contract with Chivers Jam factory to supply them with a ton. They would pay £100 for that, which doesn't sound much nowadays, but it was far more than the wholesaler had been paying towards the end of the season.

Another thing which annoyed us about the loads going to the wholesaler was that they paid by the lorry-load; the same price no matter how carefully they had been picked and presented.

We had no contract or agreement with the agent to sell everything through him, but one afternoon he announced, 'I hear you have been selling strawberries through other outlets. If you don't sell all of them through me, I shan't take any of your produce.'

Eugene was still recovering from pneumonia at the time and was resting, so this gentleman probably thought he could bully me on my own. When he arrived the next afternoon, I had all his empty flower boxes outside.

'OK,' I said. 'You can take them all away. We will sell through any outlet we choose.' I was wondering what on earth we would do if he carried out his threat, as it was the middle of the season, no time to stop for anything. However, he hastily climbed down and we never had any more trouble with him. He was a big noise in the Salvation Army.

As well as taking strawberries to Cambridge Auction Market, we discovered there were markets at Hitchin, St Neots and Saffron Walden. Few strawberries were grown near these markets, so I had them much to myself. Any auction markets north of Cambridge would be in growing areas and so prices would be low. Saffron Walden was on the same day as St Neots and much smaller. The auctioneer also got greedy and wanted 20% commission instead of the normal 10%, so Saffron Walden was dropped. Hitchin was a thirty-five mile drive each way, but well worth it. They sold a few punnets at a time and got far more than the extra 2d a pound that would make the journey worth it. I would get them there by 6.30 in the morning and be home before the rush hour.

There are always a few sharks hovering around to try to catch you out. As I drove in to Cambridge Market when we first started, they would come up to me and try to buy direct off the van. I told them that I was on the auctioneer's premises, and they would have to buy them off him. They could do this if they were in a hurry, but would have to pay whatever the top auction price was for that day. We usually did get top prices anyhow. There were many far better growers than we were with a lifetime's experience, but we got a reputation for not 'topping'. What you saw on top went down to the bottom of the pack, whether strawberries or potatoes, cauliflowers and anything else. It takes ten years to build a reputation and ten minutes to lose it.

One crafty woman thought she could do better than standing around and buying ours at top prices. She came and offered to buy all we could let her have for 9d per pound. She said Chivers were only giving 6d per pound. Unknown to her, we had a contract with Chivers at just under a shilling a pound. We also contacted many of the colleges and hotels in Cambridge. Before it was burnt down, the Garden House Hotel took quite a few. The chef said they were very good but expensive. I explained to him that we needed to make a living. The only well-known college we had any luck with was Newnham. I was very puzzled that they only wanted strawberries on Saturdays. The mystery was solved one day when I was taken to the bursar's office to collect money owed to us.

I was announced by my escort. 'Here is the young lady from Hackers,' she said.

Then I knew what was going on. Hackers were well established growers of soft fruit years before we came on the scene (our good friend George Hacker was related to them, and there wasn't much he didn't know about soft fruit). Hackers had plenty of fruit in the week, but needed all they could get for the public at weekends.

Chivers Factory foreman told us to take our offerings to them in the afternoons, after the lorries had unloaded. They came from Wisbech and surrounding areas, rattling past in the early mornings. Each of Chivers' metal trays held about fifteen pounds of fruit. Sometimes I would arrive with only about ten trays. Partly to tease me, and also the students who were earning themselves a few bob working there in the vacation, the foreman would sing out 'STRAWBERRIES!' and a couple of young chaps would come charging out on forklifts, expecting to unload tons from a lorry. The practice had stopped before we came to Histon, but local people had been allowed to bring just a few pounds at a time from their gardens. They were given chits and at the end of the season went up some wooden steps to a small office where they collected the cash owed them. I suppose Chivers thought they should support the locals.

Hearing a knock, I opened the back door one afternoon to find a very large man in a kaftan with a string of beads round his neck.

As I opened my mouth to say, 'No, thank you' to whatever he was offering, he said,

'Arjuna sent me.'

There can be very few people in Cambridge with an interest in organic food who wouldn't know the Arjuna shop. It had then just started up, being run as a restaurant in the 1960's. I had found out about them when I approached a stall on Cambridge market selling organic food. In those days it was simply for the floppy hat and sandaled brigade, looked on with suspicion by the general public. Always on the lookout for more outlets, I had said they might be interested in some of our produce. Although we had to use herbicides, as otherwise we couldn't cope with the weeds, we avoided pesticides as being potentially dangerous. Many growers had the idea that if you didn't drop down dead immediately, it was safe. One day at

Hitchin market I met an old man who had just brought in a load of gooseberries. Mildew can be an awful nuisance on them. The old way was to pick them, place them on a large sheet, then roll them backwards and forwards to rub the mildew off. I asked this man if he had any trouble.

'Oh no, I sprayed them,' he replied. I asked him what he had used. He had no idea, someone just sold it to him, saying it would work and it did. Many of these sprays were not supposed to be used within a certain period before picking.

The reason Arjuna flourished, unlike many similar projects, is that it was set up by a young man called Patrick, and was properly organised from the start. When I got to know him, I told him that he had the Midas touch; everything he started up worked. Both he and Peter, the man in the kaftan, had what I called the 'Patty Hearst syndrome'. Patty Hearst was the daughter of a very wealthy American tycoon. She was kidnapped by a gang with the Robin Hood attitude of robbing the rich to give to the poor. Their plan to get a ransom from her father was somewhat spoiled by Miss Hearst, who joined the gang, renouncing her wealth and becoming more of a drop-out than any of them.

Patrick's grandfather had made his fortune from jute. A friend calling at the family home was amazed to have the door opened by a butler. Peter's mother's riches came from African diamonds. Many communes sprung up with members denouncing their materialistic upbringing. Everybody was going to share. What is mine is yours, and what is yours is mine. The only problem was that they didn't have anything. We had one of these communes a few houses away from us. One of them made excellent bread. I was somewhat dubious about eating it, as he looked as if he was in the last stages of tuberculosis. One day this bread maker came and asked if he could borrow our van.

Eugene with 'Aunty' the van

We hastily informed him that we needed it all the time.

Peter proved to be very useful to us, taking a good quantity of our produce to restaurants and wholefood shops in London. One day he came back to tell us that they were complaining about 'the fairies' which were flying off our cauliflowers. We explained that if they didn't want sprays used, they could expect whitefly.

Peter decided to get married. He asked us to supply strawberries for his 'reception'. This took the form of a picnic on the banks of

79

the Cam. They got married in the registry office and then held a celebration in the small unused church on Castle Hill. When I went to meet them, Peter said, 'Look what I've got for the wedding.' And, rather to my consternation, he pulled up his kaftan. He was sporting a natty pair of pure white shorts that he'd bought from Marks & Spencer's. The price tag was still dangling down the side of them. I asked him if he was planning to return them after the wedding.

When Peter collected produce from us to go to London, his wife would often stay to pick fruit such as raspberries. In due course a little daughter arrived, who used to then come with them. She was a very intelligent child and could be left happily playing on her own while her mother worked. One day when Peter came to collect them, I thought I heard her say, 'Daddy mend plant.'

After they had gone, I went to investigate. I had a very small Crassula – Money Plant. Its large fleshy leaves had been too much of a temptation for the little one and she had picked them off one by one, leaving a bare stem sticking up!

CHAPTER 9
Pick Your Own and Door-to-Door

Chivers Farms had been growing strawberries for decades on a large scale. They had an army of pickers. Many did it for a living, travelling round to follow the harvesting of various crops throughout the season. Others, such as students, might just do it for a bit of pocket money, for this was all that a non-expert would make, as it was all piece work. When I was a student in the Land Army in the summer of 1947, several of us would cycle over from Newton to put in an hour or two. We were each allocated a row, and the foreman strode up and down to make sure you cleared the row, and didn't just pick the ones that were the easiest to see. You had to keep your eye on the other pickers. We picked into chip baskets which held three or four pounds of fruit. If you took your eyes off your basket, you would turn round to find it empty. Quick as lightning they were, you never saw them do it. You got no sympathy from the foreman, he knew that these 'professionals' were his best pickers.

When you first start any bending work, such as strawberry picking, it is sensible to do it for only a short time. One of my colleagues from work came out to help us one weekend. The following morning she couldn't walk up the stairs. A neighbour told us about her daughter, who was on vacation from university. They lived in March at the time. There were strawberry growers round there looking for pickers. When she came home the first evening, she was delighted and was planning what she was going to do with all the money she would earn. When she came home the second day, she was very quiet. On the third evening, she staggered in announcing, 'I am never, ever, going strawberry picking again.'

Fortunately for us, Chivers did not start P.Y.O. (Pick Your Own) until after we had given up growing them. It was an idea that was in its infancy. While we had the contract with Chivers' jam factory, we could clear our crop. One spring we heard a rumour that they were not going to take local fruit. I rang the buyer. He confirmed our suspicions, although he said he had only just been told himself. However he would still take ours if we sent them up to Wisbech where they would be bulked up! We thanked him for the offer but declined.

That was when we decided to give P.Y.O. a go. I had attended painting classes in the winter evenings and had a number of pieces of hardboard, on which were some of my efforts. I simply turned them over, wrote appropriate wording on the reverse side, and stood them up outside the gate. Thereafter I felt justified in saying that I had made several hundred pounds from my paintings!

We were in a bad position with regard to parking, having nowhere for people to draw off the busy road, but a good position to catch passers-by. Pickers come in all shapes and sizes, and varying ideas of how to get strawberries off the plants. Some people expected them to jump into the containers on their own, and would grumble that there were none there. One man came with two grown-up daughters. I thought they were taking a long time round at the back of the greenhouse before they brought them in for weighing. When they had gone, I went to have a look. The ground was covered with white fruit. The girls hadn't realised they had to be at least partly pink.

The families we dreaded most were those with toddlers whose parents made no effort to control them. It is amazing how many pounds of strawberries can be pounded to mulch under the stamping feet of a two-year-old. Not only that, but however careful you are there is always some way a determined child can hurt itself. We tried to be very polite when we suggested it might be easier for them if one parent sat in the car with 'the little one as she/he might wander into the stinging nettles/run back to the road/eat a strawberry a bird had contaminated' – or anything else I could think of. I always reminded people that birds flocked onto the plants whenever we were not about and recommended they should wash the berries before eating them. This, I hoped, would put people off scoffing too many as they picked.

Some people knew exactly how much they wanted, be it to make jam or just to eat fresh. However, many got what we called 'picking mania'. They just didn't seem to know how and when to stop. One little Burmese lass picked at least twenty pounds. We asked her what she was going to do with them.

'Oh,' says she, with a happy smile, 'I'm going to give them to my mother-in-law to make jam.'

'Does she know?' we enquired.

'Oh no,' she replied. 'It will be a lovely surprise.'

Twenty pounds of strawberries on a Sunday evening? I wonder.

One of the Senior Research Officers of the Farm Economics Branch, who was a Catholic, on hearing that I was leaving to help Eugene on our holding, suggested I contact St Edmunds House on Mount Pleasant, Cambridge. At one time, in common with many of the colleges, they had had their own gardeners to grow produce, but no longer. The household was run by several nuns with help from Irish and Spanish girls. The nuns told me that these girls were always falling out. It seems the Spanish young ladies had come mainly to learn English, and were not very workish. On special occasions fabulous silverware would be used, and the nuns produced fine meals.

We took them strawberries one day, and I am sure they said they were going to pour brandy over them. On another day they asked if we had some strawberries. I said that the season had finished but we had raspberries. They said raspberries would be fine. They wanted them for the next day. I explained that we wouldn't be able to get them picked by then. They offered to come themselves. I really think they enjoyed the outing. I remarked to a neighbour that I hoped they didn't get juice on themselves.

'Well,' I said, 'I don't want a garden full of nuns with dirty habits.' I didn't tell them, but I think they would have appreciated the joke.

We had strawberries in the field as well as near the house. One day I directed a couple of cars down there, telling the occupants I would be with them shortly. It was a good job I wasn't busy. When I got there, they had migrated across to our neighbour's strawberries. As it was a Saturday, he wouldn't be picking any until the Sunday, so these enterprising families had spotted that his rows had more ripe berries on them. I hastily got them back onto our land. I offered profuse apologies to our neighbour the next day. Fortunately he was very understanding about it, but it was the last time we sent unsupervised members of the public down there.

One Sunday afternoon a family arrived in a dilapidated old car. There were four of them – Granny and a boy of about eight in the back, and the two enormously fat parents in the front. They drove down to the field. The man and his wife got out, Granny and the boy wisely stayed put. They were not dressed for work, let alone picking strawberries in the middle of a field. He had on a suit, and wifey was dressed in bright pink, even her high-heeled shoes were pink. They got so carried away with 'picking mania' that they didn't seem to notice when a thunderstorm started. The pink lady was a sight to behold. Her dress clung so that she could hardly move, and her hair spiralled down all over her face. The husband slipped on the wet ground and sat down with a hefty thump on a goodly quantity of the strawberries he had picked. They were an extraordinary couple. They were not a bit fazed, and drove away smiling happily. I had the feeling that they were the sort, that far from making a mountain out of a molehill, would make a molehill out of a mountain.

Where I was born there was no need for door-to-door selling of food, as there were good retail shops less than half a mile away. Butcher, baker, grocer, fishmonger and two greengrocers. Milk was delivered daily and the newspaper boy came cycling past, aiming to hurl the newspapers into the porch outside the front door, but which often landed in a puddle. I would hear my father's comments when he discovered this and would come downstairs to discover the newspaper drying on the guard in front of the fire. Errand boys came with orders, either phoned in or left at the shop. As there were few fridges and no freezers, perishable things such as meat had to be bought as needed.

When my grandparents retired, they went to live in the country. A small post office and general store was about one-and-a-half miles away. To get to a main shopping area they would have had to go the three or four miles into Tring. Granddad walked to the post office once a week to collect their pension which, for the two of them, was ten shillings a week, and in those days would have bought about ten pounds of best butter. Granny never went shopping, everything came to the door. For some years they were almost self-sufficient, with poultry for eggs and meat, goats for milk, and most of their own vegetables. However, when they got too old to produce much for themselves, milk and bread came on a standing order, a greengrocer called at a regular time twice a week, the grocer came with their order once a week, and collected the order for the following week. I think the butcher came twice a week with whatever they had ordered the time before. He had to come frequently due to the lack of means to keep meat fresh for long. He drove a small high-standing cart with large wheels. It was designed for speed, not weight carrying. His horse was a lightly built, very smart animal which trotted along at a spanking pace. I determined to drive a butcher's cart as soon as I was old enough.

Up until the 1939–45 war, when a woman got married she gave up work except in very rare circumstances, or if she was very poor and needed the few extra shillings to be had from charring. So someone was nearly always at home. By 1960, when we acquired our holding, this had all changed. One or two door-to-door greengrocers were still around, but they could only operate in the evenings or on Saturdays because this was the only time they would find people at home. A Mr Wiseman from Cottenham was one of them. He drove a small flat-bedded lorry on which was stacked his wares, much of which he grew himself. He didn't grow raspberries, and had quite a few of ours. When he wanted something from the far side of his lorry, he would walk out into the road, rarely bothering to check the traffic, assuming drivers would give the parked lorry a wide berth. I warned him about it, and am sure other people did too, but he took no notice. Going round on summer evenings is one thing, but it is very different in the winter. One foggy evening the inevitable happened. He wasn't killed, but very badly injured.

As strawberry time coincided with long light evenings, we decided to see what would happen if we tried taking a few punnets round the local housing estates. We rather thought people would just laugh and say they had strawberries coming out of their ears, as so many were grown round here at the time. We were amazed; in most cases we were welcomed with not only open arms, but open purses. Often I would get a student on vacation to come round with me, and work up both sides of a street at once. They were usually quicker than I was, because I would stop too often to chat. It took me some time to get the patter right, at first I went into too much unnecessary detail. We charged the prices for strawberries that the local shops were selling them for. Retailers are naturally annoyed if they are undercut, and we wanted to make as much as possible anyway. Quite a few householders would say they had seen strawberries at the side of the road for much less. I then asked them if they had stopped to look at the sample, which might be badly picked, bird-pecked, small, little things or rotten. Ours were big and juicy and of very good flavour. Furthermore, if they could find a rotten one, I would give them a punnet free.

At one house the door was opened by a girl of about eleven or twelve and her little brother of three or four. I was just wearing a polo shirt and jeans. The jeans were rather long, so I had pulled my socks up over the bottoms of them. The little lad danced up and down with excitement. 'Strawberry man, mummy,' he called to her. She came to the door. When she saw me she laughed, and she and big sister went to get some money. The little fellow looked at me with a very solemn face. He realised he had said something funny, but didn't know what. I could see the cogs working in his brain.

After a considerable pause, he said in a very deep voice, 'You are not a man, are you?' When I agreed that this was correct, he said, 'So why are you wearing socks?' I wondered how long it was before he found a more reliable way to tell the sexes apart!

Any land we hadn't got allocated to other crops, we put potatoes in. They were known as a 'cleaning crop', not because, as some thought, they got rid of weeds on their own. Potatoes like deep cultivation, which meant that weeds would be ploughed well down. After planting they would be hoed until the tops of the plants met over the rows. From then on they were big enough to stop weed seedlings developing. Having only a few tons of spuds to sell, at first we just took them to Cambridge Auction Market. The price was so poor that we decided to sell direct to the public, not by putting them out at the side of the road, but by going round from door-to-door.

On Fridays after Christmas, when all the other crops had been harvested, we would go into the potato shed and bag up twenty half-hundredweight bags. Saturdays we would go out to sell these from door-to-door. One area we went round we referred to as 'going round the trees'. This was a recently built estate where the front of the houses faced an empty expanse of grass, and the backs led down cul-de-sacs which ended in a small circle of cobble stones, in the middle of which was planted a pathetic lonely tree.

I used to call at each house via a tall back gate into a yard surrounded by high walls, before knocking at the back doors. If an unfriendly dog was in the yard, I would chicken out. Eugene would just march in and never had any trouble. One day as I approached the door, I noticed a Siamese cat stalking me on the top of the wall. It was lucky for me the householder was in.

She said, 'He won't allow anyone to come in here.' To be attacked by a dog is one thing, but to have your eyes torn out by a cat is something else.

Having got a sale, Eugene would carry in the bag of potatoes. If I got ahead of him, I would carry them in myself. I got much amusement from pretending I was carrying a bag of feathers, then dumping the bag into the unsuspecting arms of some bloke who never normally lifted anything heavier than a briefcase. The way their knees sagged and the surprise on their faces was very entertaining.

In those days we charged £1 a bag for a half-hundredweight (25kg) of potatoes. As with the strawberries, some people would say they had seen them at the side of the road out in the Fens for much less.

'OK,' I would reply. 'Get the car out and go and fetch them.' That nearly always worked.

Sometimes a door would be opened by a small child from somewhere on the sub-continent of India. This child would call back into the recesses of the house in a language I couldn't understand. A little, wizened old woman of about 190 years old would appear.

I would say, 'Potatoes, £1 a bag.'

'80 pence,' she would say.

'No, they are £1. Take it or leave it.'

A middle-aged man would materialise behind her, rolling up a sleeve. I would start to laugh. By the time they had all gathered round the van, me asking if they wanted me to tip out a bag to save the gentleman having to dive down to see if he could find out what rubbish was hidden at the bottom, we were all in hysterics.

I arrived at one house one day to be told, 'I don't want any more potatoes from you – you put a bucketful of small ones at the bottom.'

'Madam,' I asked her, 'have you been picking out the bigger potatoes from the bags?'

She nodded.

'Then where did you expect the small ones to end up?'

CHAPTER 10
Other Crops

When the soft fruit season finished at the end of July, many growers moved on to picking plums. The area was renowned for its orchards, especially plums, for which the soil and climate were well suited. Early Rivers were followed by Czars. Later Victorias, Laxtons and Marjorie Seedlings. A quantity of Yellow Egg Plums were also grown. These were ideal for bottling but, if left to get ripe, eating them was like chewing wet blotting paper. They were canned by Chivers. As they had to be picked at exactly the right time, we were told that Chivers' buyer used to go round and tell the growers the exact day the plums had to be picked.

We only had a few plum trees, plenty for us and a few over, but not enough to matter how and where we sold them.

We learnt an interesting lesson on the approach retailers took from the several greengage trees we had. These were small, round fruit, delicious when ripe, much appreciated by our dog, who ran down to see if he could find any that had dropped off. In those days, when produce was seasonal, the earliest fruit to arrive in the market always got the best price. It was quite strange how it worked. Take rhubarb (outdoor) as an example. At the start of the season there was only a small difference between the price the grower got and the retail price. As supplies increased, both retail and producer prices dropped, but not at the same rate. The difference between the amounts widened.

Finally the retailer price levelled out, but the growers' receipts continued to fall. The retailers obviously realised that below a certain level the consumer would not buy any more, so there was no point in lowering the price. I often wondered why the growers' price kept going down. Was supply still increasing? In which case, what happened to the surplus?

Returning to our experience with the greengages, we found that if we sold them ripe, but in no way over-ripe, we would only get half the price that we got by selling them unripe, still hard and green. We came to the conclusion that the retailer would have to sell them within a couple of days, whereas he could keep unripe ones much longer. They would eventually get soft, but never develop any real flavour. I often wonder whether this had a lot to do with the demise of the plum trade. There were other reasons, one was that the prices growers received hardly covered picking costs, and pickers were getting more difficult to find. Also the government, in its wisdom, gave growers grants to grub up 'old orchards'. They probably imagined that young trees would replace them. However, when we first joined the Common Market, the price of barley was so high that all the old growing areas were turned over to grain. Even we grew a few acres of spring barley for a few years, when we were becoming semi-retired before finally giving up the holding. As we had few plums to pick, we wanted another crop to follow the soft fruit. We decided on runner beans. Our idea was to grow them up supports, as we had a happy dream of having something we could actually stand upright to pick. We bought 8 foot long T-bars, and holes were drilled a few inches from the top and three feet from the bottom. Having driven them into the ground at intervals, we threaded wire through at top and bottom. Then we spent a pleasant hour or two, throwing a large ball of string to each other over the wires. Eugene said it reminded him of when he played volleyball. We put in the beans and they duly started to climb upwards. That was when George Hacker said he thought it might be too exposed and windy. Of course, he was quite right.

We watched the plants winding their way up the strings and waited for the beans to arrive. This they did in due course, but, just as George had predicted, they flapped about against the supports and got windburn. Bang went our idea of getting our heads above our bottoms. What to do now? Unwins had a special bush variety, but we decided against them. We thought we would get an earlier and bigger yield from a normally growing variety. We decided to pinch the tops out once and give them some support to help keep them off the ground. We had a quantity of four foot iron rods left which were normally used to support wire netting round the field. There were plenty of them, so we ran a strand of wire along about two feet off the ground. Although this helped, we could not call them 'stick beans', i.e. grown up supports, so they made much less per pound. We planted three rows together. Eugene was left handed, which was useful, as we could work up the rows from each side. It was essential to get crops as early as possible to get good prices. The beans took three weeks to come up from planting. Our land was not in a hollow, it might even have been a few inches above sea level, which counts as a hill in Cambridgeshire; in fact I think it was known as Barrow Hill. This meant that we didn't suffer from ground frosts. So we risked putting the seed in in the middle of April. Just before they were due to emerge, we would spray with 'paraquat' to destroy the weed seedlings. Before we started doing this the crop would be buried in weeds, needing hours to clear.

Barley crop

The first beans would start before the end of July. We would pick them until the end of August when the price dropped dramatically; the rest would be left for seed. This saved us a lot of money as seeds were expensive. Although we still had to hunch our backs, runner beans can be picked quite quickly. The two of us would usually pick about three hundredweight a day. We tried a small patch of French beans, but they were very fiddly in comparison and only made the same price, so we soon gave up growing them.

After the end of August we still had marrows, and then started on cauliflowers. The length of their season depended on when severe frosts started. With luck we could be cutting up until Christmas.

For a few years we had grown marrows, but when courgettes became popular we switched over to them. The greenhouse, unheated, was used to bring these seedlings on. The seeds were sown in compost in three-inch peat pots. Planting these out was when we learnt that it is not true that they can be put straight into the ground. The first year we did this, the pots dried up and became so hard that no roots could penetrate them. We lost the lot. After that we always tore the pot open so that the growing plant could push it out of the way. They were, of course, well soaked before planting.

When sowing the seeds I would fill a large zinc bath with peat. This bath came from when my mother had an early washing machine where you had to rinse the clothes in a separate vessel, the bath being provided for this purpose. I would put it in the shelter we had built from windows scavenged from the old prefab houses being demolished. These had been put up after the war as quick-to-build, cheap accommodation, until better more permanent housing could be built. I would sit comfortably on a pouffe with seeds, trays and pots close at hand. A quite relaxing occupation, slightly spoiled by the peat dust floating off the pots, which irritated my breathing apparatus. One day, however, the calm was interrupted by, of all things, a tiny robin. The strawberry-picking trolleys were upended, leaning against the walls of the shed opposite where I was sitting. A robin flew up and perched on one of them, hopping up and down, and looking at me in a very agitated way. Surely, I thought, there can't be a nest in here? I got up and checked. There was, with one egg in it. I hastily removed all my paraphernalia, and went to sit in the cold (it was still only March) under the cherry tree. Later I crept back to look in the nest. There were two eggs in it.

We had neighbours who put marrow seeds directly in the ground. There were several reasons why we went to the trouble of putting them in pots to plant out. The time of planting out could be controlled, to be as early as possible whilst avoiding frosts. We got caught one year. Just as we had put out the courgettes, an air frost was forecast. Ground frosts didn't affect us as we were not in a hollow, but this was different, we could lose the whole crop. What to do? We had got punnets ready for the strawberry season. To try to protect the young plants we ran down the rows, popping a punnet over each plant. It saved the plants, but they took a long time to catch up. Being a bit too early didn't work that year. George told us that if the rooks see a dead marrow or similar plant that appears dead, they will pull it up. Dead plant? Something must be nibbling the roots. Let's have a look, it could be our dinner. The other reasons for starting the seeds in pots was that there would not be any gaps. Also, just before putting the plants out you could quickly rotovate over the whole area to get rid of weed seedlings. Thereafter one hoeing would be enough.

We discovered that, provided the pots were soaked before planting out, the soil could be as dry as dust. We had no irrigation. We had looked into getting it, but it would have been far too costly. One year it was so dry that the fertiliser we sprinkled round each plant never completely disappeared for months, but they still grew well. Sunshine and warm nights is what they need. You could draw a graph of night temperatures from the yield. The marrow family may not need to be watered, because the plants have an amazing capacity to obtain all they need from the soil. They have more suction than a herd of elephants. One year we had a few courgette plants over, and we put them in a corner next to a row of cauliflowers. Because of the shape of the field, half the cauliflowers were next to courgettes and half were not. Although they were at least a yard apart, the former were completely ruined by the greedy courgettes. They didn't actually die, but not one was worth cutting. Our friend George came over, looked at them and said, 'Those are expensive courgettes!' As winter approached the yield would drop dramatically and the first sharp frost would finish them off.

At first we grew just a few rows of cauliflowers to try them out. Someone recommended the variety All the Year Round. It was very nearly useless. Then we discovered the Australian varieties, which I believe were only available through seedsmen supplying commercial growers. We grew the varieties Kangaroo, Barrier Reef and Canberra, which matured in that order to spread the season right through from late summer to Christmas, if Jack Frost didn't come visiting.

The cauliflower seeds were sown directly into a seed bed in the field, surrounded by chicken wire to keep out any nosey birds or mammals. When they were ready for planting out, we soaked them in the rows. As we grew between 12-15,000, it would have been impossible to water them by hand after planting. Even planting them in a dry soil we had very few losses.

At first we tried marking out the rows using one of the two-wheeled tractors. It was not satisfactory, so we simply adopted the usual garden method of putting down a string line. The only difference was that each row was 150 yards long. Eugene had a long-handled dibber to save bending, and I walked backwards, dropping a plant in each hole. Eugene then firmed it in with his foot as he moved forward. This was similar to the method used in Cornwall when planting our cow cabbages to feed the stock in winter. There a mattock was used instead of a dibber. If the ground was hard, the 'dropper' needed to keep well out of reach of the mattock. Planted that way the young cabbages sloped forwards, but they soon pulled themselves upright. I was told that if you started each row from the same end of the field, instead of working up and down, it was possible to put a roller over them to firm them in. Two people were expected to plant 4,000 plants a day by this method. One local man we mentioned this to scoffed at it, and said he had planted 17,000 one day all on his own. All I can say is that it must have been a very long day. Even popping a plant in every second or two would have taken hours. We were quite happy doing 4,000 a day, thank you very much.

There were two major pests to consider with the caulis. Firstly pigeons might strip them. We found a spray called 'Avitech' which was supposed to deter them, and we used this when we could get hold of it. Whether it worked or whether the birds were not interested, we never knew. Cabbage root fly was the other problem. We went to a talk about it. We were told that the sprays needed were so lethal that they should really only be applied by a fully kitted-out contractor. (The talk was being sponsored by a contractor.) Right at the end of the notes we were given was a paragraph which said that if no sprays were used, ninety per cent of the fly eggs would be eaten by ground beetles. (They would be killed by the sprays.) However, the best advice we had was not to transplant when the Cow Parsley (Queen Anne's Lace) was in flower. This had nothing directly to do with the root fly, but conditions which suited the parsley also suited the fly and coincided with the laying of the root fly eggs. Thereafter we avoided transplanting when the Cow Parsley was in flower and never had any trouble.

Another problem at that time was that after combining, nearly all the straw was burnt. Bits of surprisingly greasy straw stuck to the heads and were very difficult to remove. Like thinking we could have an easy standing-up job picking the beans, we got caught out by thinking we could use the tractor to pull the cut heads off the field. The tractor was just not man enough to pull the smart little trailer we purchased for the purpose. It was relegated to the back of the shed and we sat on it when we had our coffee. A very expensive seat. So we were reduced to hauling the caulis by wheelbarrow. On a wet Sunday hauling out over six hundred, thirty at a time, was not exactly the way we would have chosen to spend the weekend, but they had to be ready for the market on Monday. Most of the cauliflowers we sent to Cambridge Auction Market, packed in paper sacks. We were careful to grade by size, so that buyers could see what they were getting. Hippy Peter, he of the kaftan, took quite a number to his customers. He reported one day that they were grumbling about the 'fairies' which were flying all over their premises. We pointed out very gently that they didn't want any sprays used, so they had to expect things like white flies.

CHAPTER 11
Some More Unusual Crops

The reason we decided not to grow asparagus, when someone asked us if we would, was not because the disaster with the salsify had put us off trying different crops. Indeed, as beginners we had little experience of growing any market garden produce, so it didn't make much difference which ones we tried. Also, we were not set in our ways as established growers tended to be. The reason for not wanting to grow asparagus was because it takes up a lot of room to get a decent amount, rather a long time to establish and has to remain in situ for years, thus depriving us of space to rotate our other crops. Also weeds could be a major problem, as herbicides were not as advanced as they are now.

Eugene's father had grown tobacco, so it was something Eugene wanted to try, as he complained that our tobacco was not strong enough. He grew a few plants, but it was not a success. If I remember correctly it was because we came up against our unreliable climate; wet when you needed sunshine to dry the leaves.

There were often good reasons why some of the crops we tried were not generally grown. They could be difficult to grow, subject to pests and diseases, and low yielding. On one of my farm visits I had been told that rooks were such a nuisance that the farmer had given up growing maize as fodder for his cattle. However, we thought we would try a small area of sweetcorn ('corn-on-the-cob') as it was popular at that time. All was well until the first green shoots appeared. 'Something interesting here,' crowed the rooks to each other. Having pulled up the leaves and discovered the juicy seed underneath, they proceeded to work their way up the rows. We might have persevered by starting the plants in pots, but as they really all had only one decent cob each, worth less than a shilling, we gave up the idea.

A couple of the oddities we tried, more for fun than anything else, were custard marrows and vegetable spaghetti. The former we called 'flying saucers' as they looked like pictures of these we had seen, only with scalloped edges. They were popular at Cambridge Auction Market, but we only grew a few as the yield was low.

The only person who showed any interest in the vegetable spaghetti was a stallholder on the Cambridge city centre market who dealt in more unusual greengrocery. I believe it was his stall that Prince Charles patronised when he was at the university. The problem with this stallholder was that he didn't arrive until late in the morning, often after everyone else had set up and vehicles had been moved away from the Market Square. I therefore had to park round a corner, and it was not long before I fell foul of a traffic warden. He was not a bit helpful when I explained my predicament. I had no choice but to tell the market man I would not be able to bring him anything. He said I could deliver to his home. I don't remember where it was, but it was miles away and he didn't buy much from us, so we didn't continue with either him or the vegetable spaghetti. We left some out in the field quite late one autumn, and the mice loved it.

We did supply one of the other stallholders with quite a lot of produce; nearly all our courgettes and a good many runner beans. Originally this man, Sid, had worked on another stallholder's land who would also send him to do cultivations for other growers. He did our ploughing. Sid's boss was a very unhappy character. I'm sure it was because he looked so miserable that the public avoided his stall. More than once I saw queues of people waiting to be served by his neighbour while standing right in front of his stall, ignoring the poor man who was sunk in perpetual gloom. Every so often I would call round to his bungalow to pay for the work his man, Sid, had done on our land.

I used to say to Eugene, 'This time I will try really hard to get him to smile.' But I never could.

One morning Sid arrived for work to find his boss had hanged himself in the garage. Sometime later a friend of ours, who was a neighbour of his, told me a bit about him. He had a brother, who was his mother's favourite. For years this brother had been in Africa, but was on his way home, to the delight of his mother, when he got ill and died. It was almost as if she blamed the son who had remained at home with her. I was told that he was hoping to marry, but she somehow put an end to that. So there he was, middle-aged and all alone after his mother died. He might have been miserable whatever the circumstances, but some mothers seem to have a capacity to destroy their sons.

Sid, a middle-aged family man, was now without a job. He applied to take over the market stall. The council did their best to block this. However, the other traders rallied round him, and he was able to carry on there making much more of a success of it. For a start, he looked exactly like Clark Gable, and who wouldn't want to buy fruit and veg from Clark Gable?

Before the war, no ordinary English cook would dream of using garlic. It was foul-smelling stuff used by those who ate frogs' legs and other unmentionables. Then, holidays began to be taken overseas by a growing number of the population. Continental cooking became the 'in thing'. A demand for garlic started. Eugene's family had grown and eaten it at home, not only as a flavouring, but to keep all ills, and probably the Devil, at bay. Eugene would gnaw away at a whole clove, especially with cold meat or sausage. Several times I woke in the night, and was halfway down the stairs thinking the gas was escaping, before I realised it was his breath. So I had to nibble a bit whether I liked it or not, so that I didn't notice his breath.

Some of Eugene's friends grew a bit in their gardens, so we thought we would give it a try. We started with just a few corms and built it up until we had about two hundredweight each year. That was enough, as we dug it by hand, and Eugene cut off the roots and tops with scissors and cleaned off the outer layer of skin, which was grey and dirty-looking. Whether it is possible to do this by machine, we never found out. When a French market came to Cambridge which had a stall selling only garlic, with their limited English and my even more limited French, it seemed that they prepared theirs by hand as we did.

You are advised to plant garlic in the autumn. We couldn't do this as the land was not cleared of other crops in time. We tried a small amount in the garden, comparing autumn and spring planting, and found it made little difference, as long as it was put in as early as possible in spring. One year bad weather held us up until late in April. The resulting corms were tiny and virtually useless.

The problem with English garlic is not growing it, it is drying it. We would take it up as soon as the tops yellowed in August. Left too late the tops would break off and the corms start to rot. We would bunch about ten together, bend the tops over, secure with a rubber band, and hang them on wires stretched across an airy shed. Garlic can't stand as much frost as onions, so in late autumn we would put them on wire racks in the greenhouse, covered if it got really cold. Although we only grew a small amount, they were a useful crop as they made good money, mostly at a whole food shop in Cambridge.

Garlic to the left, courgettes to the right

What inspired us to grow pumpkins I can no longer remember. They turned out to be one of our most useful crops. They were easy to grow, using the same method as for the courgettes. Once planted, a single hoeing and that was all they required until the threat of frosts reminded us to harvest them. The large yellow flowers were much appreciated by all kinds of insects, including bumble bees. When harvested we piled them up in a shed, covering them with layers of sacking if it got cold. We sold a few to local shops. Hippy Peter took a good many, and the rest went all the way up to Bradford through the Cottenham agent, a much nicer man than the one with whom we had had problems. They made good money for something so trouble-free. What the customers did with them we never fathomed, probably mostly soup. We followed a recipe for pumpkin pie. We were not fussy eaters, but offered most of it to the dog, who took one sniff and stalked away. However we were given a recipe for a preserve which could be used instead of the usual mincemeat at Christmas. It consisted of cubed pumpkin, dried fruit, demerara sugar, and – the expensive bit – preserved ginger. Put in a Kilner jar, it would keep for months. Eugene said that when he was at home they only used them for cattle feed. To have packed things of that size in crates would have cost too much, so we put about three at a time in paper sacks. Getting these to balance long enough on the potato weigher would try anybody's patience. Each year the agent would say the transport driver complained that they rolled off the pallets, and asked us to please put them in crates. We would nod and smile, and quietly forget about it. The only time the bags seemed to roll off was at the end of October just before Halloween! We found the pumpkins would keep very well until Christmas, and then would start to rot.

As soon as Eugene reached sixty-five, we started to cut down on the work. I never mentioned it to him, but I knew there was no way he could offer proof of age from his place of birth, and communications had ceased long since. A man he knew had contacted his mother, and she and his brother had been promptly sent off to a concentration camp, such was Stalin's paranoia. Fortunately Eugene had kept his Army pay book and documents from when he had first been called up. The Pensions Department accepted the date of birth recorded on them.

The first crop we discarded was strawberries. Not so much because of picking, but they needed a lot of time weeding and controlling them all the year. Apart from veg for ourselves, we gradually cut down to just courgettes for Sid, pumpkins and scabious, which was always useful as there was never a glut; just a few flowers at a time right through the summer and autumn.

Britain had by this time joined the Common Market. It was the time of the 'Barley Barons'. The price was so good it was even worth putting our few acres into spring barley. We couldn't put in winter barley, because we had to get the land ready after other crops. I loved watching it waving in the breeze when the heads were still green, shimmering with gold. It was when it got ripe that the fun started. We had to get three things in synchronisation – the weather, our neighbour with his combine, and a trailer supplied by the corn merchant into which to put the grain ready for collection. Naturally our neighbour would only come if he had nothing of his own ready for cutting. Getting a trailer was generally the most difficult. Many farmers would order them before they were needed to make sure they had them, and they would sit there for days. The grain merchant would tell me to ring at 6.30 in the morning to see if they could supply one that day.

Our neighbour often said, 'There is no need to ring me to ask me to come with the combine, I will see if the trailer is there.'

We knew that before long the corn merchant would no longer require our few tons of barley. We had sold the house and garden in 1980, and the field in 1985, just retaining an allotment-sized bit to grow our own vegetables. We had been running the holding for twenty-five years. We could have expanded, in fact we did get to view more land on several occasions. However, it would have meant having to employ more staff, and I would have ended up doing mainly office work, to avoid which I had wanted to have the holding in the first place. It depends on the individual, but both of us preferred being self-employed. Your success or failure is then in your own hands, and you can work as many or as few hours as you wish. You can't be sacked, but if you don't work, you won't eat.

CHAPTER 12

Barbus

The cat my mother brought to us, because she couldn't keep him, could have wandered for miles from the back of the house without coming to a road, and with fields and orchards to hunt in. But, contrary as all cats are, he had to go out the front and cross the busy road. He got away with it for two years, until the inevitable happened. We decided that a dog could be more easily safeguarded. It was 1966, and I was leaving the Farm Economics Branch, so would be at home to look after a dog. A Miss Duff rescued stray dogs and tried to re-home them. She had a stall in Cambridge Market to try to make enough to pay for their keep at kennels outside Cambridge. I rang her up and she said I could go and see if I liked the look of any of the ones there. These strays were in pens away from other dogs, as they were most likely not inoculated, and could be carrying all sorts of diseases. As I approached the pens, one terrier flew at the door, snarling in a fashion that meant business, so I moved on. A fairly large animal, about the size of a Labrador but not so chunky, came to the front of his pen, looking delighted to be noticed. He was white with fox-brown patches, and was very pretty. Perhaps pretty doesn't sound quite right for a male animal, but he *was* very good-looking.

The man who ran the kennels asked me if I would like the dog let out so that I could have a good look at him. Released from his prison, the poor chap didn't know whether to rush up to greet me or to go over to the nearest bunch of nettles to empty his bladder. He chose the latter. I could almost see the look of relief about him as he then threw himself excitedly in my direction. I thought that whatever else might be wrong with him he was at least house-trained.

'Think you'll like him?' asked the man. I nodded. 'Well, why don't you take him now?'

I said I didn't have any sort of lead, but that was no problem I was assured, and a piece of rope was produced and carefully knotted round his neck. Well, he was as wild as a curlew. Put in the back of the van, he tied himself up Houdini-fashion with the rope. I reckon the kennel man was glad to have found someone to take the animal off his hands. On the way home I had to stop to buy a collar and heavy chain to prevent him strangling himself. When I got home I presented him with some trepidation to Eugene. To make him think the dog belonged to him, I said, 'What would you like to call him?'

After a little thought, Eugene said, 'We had a dog called Barbus at home. Let's call him that.'

Barbus was the dog who had warned them when some men came in the night with the intention of smashing up their threshing machine.

The first thing Barbus did when I got him in the house was try to climb on my lap, all fifty-odd pounds of him. He had been taught silly things like sitting up to beg, but nothing useful like coming when he was called. I guess he had been a beautiful cuddly puppy whose owners couldn't cope with his exuberance when he got big.

Although he was full of life, Barbus was rather thin, and had the appearance of having tried to fend for himself for some time. We decided to get him checked over by the vet, and given vaccinations. When it came to putting 'breed' on the vaccinations certificate, the vet hesitated, looking thoughtful.

'I suppose,' she said, 'we had better put him down as a Retriever Cross.'

That was true, as he was never happy unless he had something to carry. What other genetic material was in his make-up defeated all attempts to fathom. There aren't many white breeds. He was about the size and shape of a Dalmatian, but he had no spots and, although short, his coat was too coarse. As for the red patches, they were so fox-like we did wonder.

Barbus was a very amiable buffoon of an animal. He loved everybody and assumed they reciprocated. Babies were his speciality. Given the chance, he would dance up and kiss them. When we had strawberries we used to tie him up to the cherry tree, and he was convinced that all the customers had come especially to see him. One evening I had let him off his lead and he was in the garden with me, when a lady came to see if she could have some fruit. She was holding a toddler by the hand. Barbus spotted them before I did, and was racing towards them before I could stop him. I shouted, but he carried on. The terrified woman grabbed her child into her arms, thinking they were being attacked. Breathless, I tried to explain he was only going to smother the child in big, slobbery licks. It was all the germs he was probably carrying that made his own enthusiastic welcomes so undesirable.

The vet decided Barbus was about 18 months old when we got him. He was still at the chewy stage. I was upstairs when I heard a slight thud, thud, from the kitchen. I ran down to discover he had only reached up to the table and helped himself to the bread knife. Luckily he was busy chewing the handle, and had managed to avoid the blade.

When I took the dog for a walk, I generally gave him something to carry. Sometimes it was an umbrella. I got considerable amusement to see him trying to manoeuvre near enough to a lamppost to cock his leg. The first time he tried to get through a door carrying his umbrella, he just went 'klonk' and stopped dead. But he soon found a way to twist his head about and manoeuvre it through.

We had only had Barbus a short time when he came trotting towards me with two tiny feet sticking from the sides of his mouth. When I opened his mouth, a fledgling robin was sitting on top of his tongue. It was somewhat ruffled and very cross, but otherwise unharmed. He had a very soft mouth until he caught his first rat, which bit him. Thereafter, when he caught a rat he would jerk it up into the air. Anyone standing nearby was in danger of it landing on their head – hopefully dead. He had a different method for everything he caught. Small fry such as mice and shrews, he would trap under his forepaws. Rabbits would be caught at the back of the neck and appeared to be pushed against the ground. I never actually saw him catch a hare, though he would occasionally appear carrying one. How he had achieved this I have no idea. A hare could be sitting a matter of thirty or forty yards away, and he would set off on its scent, oblivious to the fact that if he had taken his nose off the ground he would have seen it. I used to ask him if he would like to borrow my glasses. When the hare decided to move, he would set off behind it, screaming with excitement. There were deep ditches all around the fields. When the hare came to one, it would leap gracefully over. Barbus would plunge down the side, splash through the water and struggle up the other side, still yelling at the top of his voice. By this time the hare would be hundreds of yards away. Eventually Barbus would come back puffing and panting, pretending he hadn't meant to catch it anyway. One day he put up a young hare in the garden. He set off, yelping as usual. After a few seconds there was silence. He appeared with his mouth stuffed full of hare. The poor silly creature must have jumped sideways – I believe it is called 'wrenching' – as its mother must have told it to, and jumped straight into the dog's mouth. A big surprise for both of them.

One evening Barbus brought a larger hare home with him. Perhaps it was too old to get away. I was discussing with him what we should do with it, when I saw a white shape in the garden. It was the white blouse which a neighbour's daughter was wearing. She had a Boxer dog by the collar, which was towing her towards us. I hastily shut our dog in the conservatory. The lass explained that they were looking after it, and it had got out. I told her I would get our dog's lead and help her get it home. We went the back way, down our garden and into theirs. In the meantime the girl's little brother came running along the road to ask us if we had seen the dog. He opened the conservatory door, and Barbus shot out. We were just about to take the Boxer into their house when I heard a noise behind us. There was Barbus, with the hare clutched firmly in his jaws. He must have wanted to see where I had gone, but was afraid to leave the hare in case somebody pinched it.

Leverets he, fortunately, never killed to my knowledge. They didn't try to run away, so he poked them with his nose enquiringly, whereupon they squealed in terror, poor little things, and I was able to drag him away before they were harmed. Anything that didn't try to escape puzzled Barbus. We were walking down to the village one evening. He was trotting on ahead. He stopped to sniff at something that was in the middle of the pathway. It was a white cat. White cats are often deaf. That one certainly was. It had no idea he was coming until he poked it. Terrified, it shot five or six feet into the air and dived into the hedge. Barbus was too mystified to go after it, which was just as well for both of them. It was facing us, eyes popping out of its skull, mouth wide open and flanks heaving. I hope it recovered.

I was walking round an orchard one evening, trespassing as usual – I blame my father for that. He would wander all over the place and if someone asked him if it was alright to go in a certain direction, he always said it was (perhaps they assumed he owned the land as he was reasonably well dressed).

Barbus showed a great interest in a large clump of nettles. To my amazement, I found a nest of tiny leverets; I think it was at least eight. I had assumed that mother hares gave birth to each leveret in a separate place, as you only ever found one at a time. Do they have them all in the same place and then carry them out to leave them individually, to save losing the whole lot to a predator?

Skylarks found our cropping to their liking, and we usually had several nests. Sometimes Barbus found them before I could stop him. The way he dealt with an egg was very clever. He didn't grab it and swallow it and smash it up. He very delicately punctured the shell and lapped up the contents before it could run out. He was also very fond of raspberries which he picked in an equally delicate manner.

We had other birds around, such as yellowhammers and lapwings at certain times. One day I noticed a little bird that resembled a smart sparrow in his Sunday best. Looking in our bird book, I decided it was a Reed Bunting. It sat there all day going, 'Cheep, cheep, Chisick.' I remarked to Eugene that I was very glad I wasn't his mate sitting on her eggs. It must have been driving her mad.

At that time we had scores of sparrows round the place. They filled the gutters of the garage with their untidy nests and perched all along the rafters inside. We ignored them until someone suggested we should plant radishes on the roof of our van.

'They should grow well with all that manure,' he remarked.

We tried to discourage them by putting sheets of corrugated iron across the rafters, but they still managed to make a mess. Every so often I would take a broom handle and rattle the corrugated iron. Sparrows would scatter in all directions. I am sorry to say that the boy sparrows seemed much brighter than the girl sparrows. The males would go straight out of the escape holes, but the females went into an hysterical panic, which caused Barbus to get very excited. He would leap about, knocking things over, in a vain attempt to catch a feathered morsel. To save the place being wrecked, I had to open the garage doors and shoo everybody out.

One sparrow we called Samson. His mate wanted to go a bit upmarket. Not for her the garage tenements. She wanted to build her residence under the washhouse roof. The only problem was that the corrugations were too small for her to squeeze under. We had a grandstand view of the proceedings from the kitchen window. She tried several times to force her way in, but had to back out, all ruffled up. She then proceeded to nag her mate – and could she nag! He tried to enlarge the hole by getting the corrugated sheet in his beak and trying to bend it. However hard he tried, it was no use. Madam would be forced to back out again in an ever worse temper. I felt so sorry for the poor little chap that I went out and levered the iron up. I bet her ladyship went round telling all the other sparrows what a fabulous position she had.

There was another enterprising bird. One morning I heard 'tap, tap, tap' coming from the conservatory. Barbus slept out there, under the bench on an old car seat. He was not a greedy dog, and often left some scraps in his bowl. A female blackbird had lined up her fledglings on the grass and was carrying out bits of dog biscuit to them. I was going to say the little birds were lined up on the lawn, but that is a misnomer. We had a small patch of rough grass at the back and a bit more at the front of the house. I could never get enthusiastic about grass unless it was to feed stock, so this grass did not receive much TLC. When we were very busy I often didn't get around to cutting it. One summer our next door neighbour, who had his house on the market, offered – in desperation – to come round to cut it, as he feared the sight might put off potential buyers. The next year I tried spraying the front over with malic acid, which was used to slow down growth. I had heard of it being used on hedges. It certainly worked on the grass as it held the grass in check. That allowed other weeds to flourish, and we had an interesting collection of plants like nipplewort. To return to the thieving blackbird, Barbus was lying on his bed only about two feet away, watching her, but making no attempt to chase her off. Whether he was being tolerant, or just knew he had no chance of catching her, I have no idea. She came every day for quite a while.

Everything would be clear and weed-free before we started harvesting the first crops, but in June and until the end of July we were too busy to keep on top of it. When we stopped to draw breath we would discover that a forest of weeds were threatening to take over. Fat hen would be romping away fine plants about two feet high. We enlisted Barbus to help with these. He needed little encouragement to 'kill' them. If they wouldn't pull up easily, he would dig all round, growling furiously, until he could yank them up. Then he would shake them vigorously, which was useful, as it got rid of all the soil. We weren't quite so pleased that we had taught him to pull up weeds one day. We heard laughter coming from the next door garden. It seems that they were digging up old cabbage stalks, and he was helping them. That was OK but he brought them all back to our garden, which meant that I had to dispose of them, much to the amusement of our neighbours.

He was not a swimming dog, but he had a habit of sinking down into puddles when he was hot. He didn't think he had been on a proper walk unless he had torn his ears scrambling about in brambles. He would then come up to us, looking very pleased with himself and shake, splattering blood all over us.

Although he was a big, strong chap, Barbus was a real wimp. He didn't like fighting, and would only retaliate if he had to. There was a big Boxer called Rusty, whose owner couldn't control or ever hold onto him, as she was rather frail. One day they met up the track known as Gun's Lane. Rusty pushed Barbus back into the ditch – fortunately dry. Barbus threw himself onto his back and waved his legs in the air. Rusty put a paw on his chest, and looked round at us.

'See, I'm the boss.'

One day we were picking up potatoes, Eugene at one end of the row and me at the other. Barbus spotted a man in the sugar beet field next to ours. The man was carrying a gun. That was enough. Whether it was the sight or the smell that unnerved Barbus, we didn't know. He came over and hid by lying down behind me. He must have thought Eugene was a better shield, because he soon got up and went to lie behind him. So much for him protecting us! In the autumn, when sugar beet was fully mature and he couldn't do it any damage, we used to let him go for a hunt round. This was as much for our amusement as for his. He would leap about three feet into the air, twisting and turning, ears flapping, to see what he could find. Once he came on a fox, which he circled round but wasn't man enough to tackle, which pleased us but not one of our neighbours when we told him, because he kept chickens.

One day our good friend, George Hacker, was discussing his old Jack Russell. He told us, 'I said to my missus, I don't mind the old dog knowing what I say, it's when he knows what I think it is getting a bit much.' Many animals seem to know what you are thinking. It is not only that they pick up tiny physical signs humans wouldn't notice, but they seem to pick up 'vibes' even if you are out of sight. We had a lean-to conservatory Eugene had built onto the back of the house. Barbus had his bed in there just outside the back door. I would go in and out on various errands, and he would take no notice of me. Then I would decide to take him for a walk. His collar and lead, and my boots and coat were all out there. Even before I had opened the back door, he would be off his bed, tail wagging, ready for the off. How did he know? Probably a good job he couldn't talk.

We enjoyed the old boy's company for over thirteen years, then he started getting lumps which proved to be cancerous. He was game to the end, a great character who lived a full doggy life.

Barbus with myself and Eugene in the orchard

CHAPTER 13
Setting Up a Smallholding Now

Tired of the hustle and bustle of the city and decided to move to the countryside and purchase some land? Perhaps crossing your mind to take up farming? With land at anything up to £7000 an acre, you will need to be a millionaire to do so. It is likely that you will have to settle for a few acres as we did.

The first thing to decide is whether you will just run the holding as a hobby, or expect to get a goodly contribution to your income from it. If the former, a picturesque area may be more important to you than good soil. For example, to the south of Cambridge it has what passes for hills in Cambridgeshire and the landscape is therefore more attractive, but the soil to the north of Cambridge is much more productive.

If, for whatever reason, you are going to keep animals, please be sure you learn as much as possible before getting your own. Reading up about them is obviously useful, but hands-on experience is a must, otherwise it is so easy to inadvertently cause problems for yourself and suffering for the animals. One of our neighbours was given a runty pig. Anyone with any knowledge of pigs would know it would never be any good. Another thing they were not aware of is that pigs must have dry floors to sleep on. A bit of straw on bare concrete is not good enough. In nature they inhabit thick undergrowth where the soil is completely dry. That pig got ill. They paid vet bills for it, which did little good as the animal would never be anything other than a pot-bellied runt.

There is another consideration before getting livestock. You can't leave them and go off on holiday, not even if you just have a few grazing animals as lawn mowers. As soon as your back is turned they will find a way to break out, get tangled in barbed wire, get on their backs (sheep) or whatever else they can think of. One dairy farmer being interviewed on television recently revealed that he had not had a holiday for 25 years. Of course, you may not have a large number of animals; a few minutes of attention a day will probably be all they will require. A reliable neighbour willing to pop in should be possible to find. But note the word 'reliable'.

Beware the over-enthusiastic 'I would love to water your plants/ feed your chickens/pigs/goats, etc'. It is one thing to come home to a greenhouse full of dead plants, quite another to find the RSPCA on your doorstep. If you want to have animals on a few acres to generate a reasonable contribution to your income, this would only be possible with livestock which could be kept in large enough numbers on a small acreage, such as poultry or pigs. These animals would depend almost entirely on bought-in feed, which is very vulnerable to the price of grain. Of course a considerable amount of the food we waste could be used for the pigs to be fed on swill, if a government inspector hadn't fallen down on his job and not taken away the licence from the farm which gave rise to the outbreak of foot and mouth disease.

Horticultural crops give a much wider choice on a small acreage. If you just want something to make a minor contribution to your income, you could grow something like asparagus, providing the soil is suitable. If you are not too far off the beaten track a worthwhile quantity of produce may be sold at the gate. Soft fruit might be another option. As the evenings are light when it is in season, going from door-to-door when people are at home can be lucrative.

However, you may be hoping to make a major part or even all of your income from your holding. At this point we will consider what we did and see whether you could approach it in the same way. We had very little capital so started slowly, one of us remaining in employment while the other partner concentrated on building up production. We worked the holding for 25 years, for about half that time we depended on it entirely for our income.

In order to get a steady income, it is desirable to be harvesting crops or selling them from storage, for as many months of the year as possible. We just had a small glasshouse, its main purpose being to propagate courgettes and pumpkins. When they were out, we generally filled it up with tomato plants we bought in, simply to make use of it. Sometimes I tried a few pot plants. Other than that, everything else was outside. The earliest crop we started to harvest was in late April/early May (Pyrethrums and Dutch Irises) and we could normally cut cauliflower up until Christmas. Pumpkins generally had to be sold off by Christmas, as we found they would not keep longer than that. For the remaining four months we had only a few potatoes and garlic to sell. It gave me time to catch up with the accounts!

As we harvested mainly one crop at a time, this was easy to organise. If we had been content to take the prices from the wholesale markets, disposal could have been very simple too. We would not even have needed a vehicle: the agent would have picked up our produce to be sent to one of the large conurbations. A local carrier would have called twice a week to take goods to Cambridge Produce Auction Market. Many growers did this, quite a few of whom were small part-timers with shift work which gave them time off in daylight hours. Often, especially with flowers and soft fruit, their wives would make themselves a bit of pin-money from the huge gardens many of them had. There are still growers with the attitude that they can simply wave goodbye to their produce at the gate. They grumbled about the ridiculous prices they often got, but argued that 'something was better than nothing'. As we were trying to make a living from our holding, this attitude was no good to us. Over the years we built up a variety of different outlets, selling each item of produce wherever it could give the best return. A list of outlets used is as follows:

a) Through agents to wholesale markets in large towns and cities such as London, Birmingham (our usual market), Manchester, Bradford (pumpkins), etc.

b) Local Auction markets: Cambridge, Hitchin, St Neots, Saffron Walden.

c) Direct to manufacturers (Chivers).

d) A small wholesaler, selling to shops and restaurants in North London.

e) Retailers

f) Direct to consumers, pick-your-own and door-to-door, a couple of colleges and one hotel.

The table below gives the approximate percentage sold via each outlet for the main crops.

CROP	A	B	C	D	E	F
Cut flowers	90	Neg	-	-	10	Neg
Soft fruit	10	40	20	10	Neg	20
Runner Beans	30	40	-	-	30	-
Courgettes	-	60	-	-	40	-
Pumpkins	50	20	-	20	10	Neg

Why did we sell where we did? Obviously because that is where we expected to make most money. Even for a small grower, as we were, we had too many bunches of flowers to sell except in bulk. This was possible only at the large markets. Because flowers were sold on a commission basis, the salesman would always get the best price he could for you. Even so, you could come unstuck as we did one year with Irises (see chapter on flowers). We only found one retailer, a florist, who would offer a good price, and he could only take a case or two each week.

For soft fruit it was essential to find outlets other than the wholesale markets in the big cities to make any sort of income. Local auction markets were good, especially as we were very careful to present a good sample and therefore generally topped the Cambridge Market. Why some growers thought the purchasers would never get to the bottom of the pack, I cannot imagine. One man told me, 'I was so fed up with the price I got for the potatoes last week, that I put a bucket of rotten ones at the bottom of each sack this time.'

Chivers Jam Factory would also take local fruit. Obviously they didn't pay the price you would hope to get for the best berries, but you knew what you were going to get, and it gave a margin over pickers' costs.

The Fen soils, a bit to the North of us, are not suitable for cauliflowers, so not many were grown in the Cambridge area. Tons of these were grown in other parts of the country, so it was not sensible to send them to big city markets. They did much better locally. Pumpkins were unique. We got a steady price for them at Bradford Market right up until Christmas. I think they would do well almost anywhere now.

So where would that leave you, starting up 40 years later? Of the outlets we used, many are no longer available. There are no longer any agents for the large city markets round here. Chivers Jam Factory is still there, but all the soft fruit is imported. To be fair, the agents were only there because there were many small growers in the area with insufficient produce to run their own transport. Also, how many growers have a jam factory on their doorstep? The local auction markets have also vanished, most of them having been built on. Cambridge has a Travel Lodge and Leisure Centre where the produce auctions took place. There is still at least one small local wholesaler and a few independent retailers – shops and market stalls – who might be interested in local produce. Also, there are now two outlets that were not available to us. While some growers sold produce from their holdings, these were in no way as organised and sophisticated as the description 'Farm Shop' implies. A word of warning may be appropriate here. A well-known grower in Cambridgeshire sold their own soft and top fruit from an uncomplicated set-up where they stored and picked their fruit. Then they went overboard setting up a state-of-the-art sales floor, selling and even bringing in all sorts of exotic produce, including pretty paper napkins and things which had nothing do with their own produce. They had no vegetables, and the ratio of their own crops reduced with time. People go to a farm shop in order to get fresh food, not fancy goods. Cash-wise, the final straw seemed to be when they filled a yard full of Christmas trees. One little boy asked his mother if they could have a tree. She looked at the ticket on one. 'Not at those prices,' she said. A couple of months later the farm shop closed down. The most exciting development for small growers is the Farmers' Market. Some are much better than others, but a good producer selling at a sensible price is unlikely to be short of customers.

What cropping regime would be best, and where would you sell the produce? It is essential to have a firm idea of outlets before planting.

If you are new to it, it would be a good idea to get in a bit of practice before approaching buyers. If you don't come up with the goods, you will be unlikely to get a second chance.

What about outdoor cut flowers? The UK has never been a good market for bunches of flowers. When I was in France in 1964, I got talking to a young woman selling from a stall. I was amazed at how much her customers were willing to pay – at least twice as much as flowers were being sold for by UK retailers.

Now many more flowers are grown under glass, and/or overseas. The simple bunches of flowers, such as Pyrethrums, Sweet Williams, Cornflowers and even Irises and Scabious, are hardly ever grown now. Supermarkets offer cut flowers, often mixed bunches, at very competitive prices and they also have a long vase life. There is no way someone starting up could compete. Also, from the table of outlets we used, you will notice that nearly all our flowers went via an agent to the big city markets. This has disappeared as an outlet. Even with our small acreage in flowers (less than two acres), our output was too large for local sales. In my view, the only way that you could make outdoor cut flowers profitable would be if you, or someone you were in partnership with, was a highly experienced professional flower arranger and could get contracts with top hotels and functions such as weddings.

Would vegetables be a better bet? Almost certainly. However, it would not be possible in the way we did it, mainly concentrating on one crop at a time. Even if you could find a local wholesaler, he would probably only have the few remaining retailers to look after, plus a possible school or two. When we had runner beans we picked three hundredweight a day, and in the cauliflower season about six hundred head. Your most likely outlet today would be a Farmers' Market. To attract customers you would need a range of produce.

No-one is going to be attracted to a stall selling only cabbages! Both to keep customers coming and to give yourself a regular income, you would need to produce as near all-the-year-round as possible. Crops such as runner beans, courgettes and cauliflowers need picking at least once a week. Some small Farmers' Markets are only held once a month. You might need to find more than one market within easy reach. Vegetables such as carrots, parsnips and leeks require washing these days. Gone are the days when a little twisted carrot covered in mud could be labelled 'organic' and expect to thrill the public.

There is a market out there waiting to be tapped. There are many households now with only one occupant. They don't all live on ready meals. Where vegetables are presented loose, the customer can pick as little as they wish. Most supermarket packs are too big for one consumer. Also, cabbages and cauliflowers are generally enormous. They could last a single person up to a week. Who wants to eat the same vegetable every day? Mini-veg seed is available. Would it be possible to build up a box scheme aimed at the single householder? The value per box would obviously be quite low, but a way might be found to deliver to a central point for collection. Perhaps this would be worth thinking about.

Schools, pubs and restaurants are far more interested in buying fresh produce nowadays. It might be possible to get contracts with them. Beware putting all your eggs in one basket, as their catering requirements could change out of the blue and you may find your produce is no longer required.

A full-blown farm shop puts you in a different league. A wide range of locally-grown produce must be available all year, usefully including animal products and homemade pickles, jams, etc. Adequate car parking is a must. A picnic area and play area for children is useful. Animals (to look at, but best not to touch – health and safety!)

will always attract family visits. Unless you have a large family all willing to help, you will have to employ staff. This can be a minefield. However, you might find an established farm shop with a gap which you could fill. If you are within easy walking distance of plentiful customers, or on a route passed regularly by commuters and with a lay-by or somewhere where they can pull in, a surprising amount of produce can be sold from a simple stall. The disadvantage is that the price would have to be lower than at the supermarket, where they could get a much wider range in one visit.

One option – and this might be the most attractive if you could wait a few years to build up production – would be for soft and top fruit. Crop-wise this would be easier to organise. It would not be necessary to offer a wide variety of produce at any one time. People will be interested in a stall just offering strawberries, for instance. The supermarkets offer soft and top fruit all the year round. Their requirements are for vast quantities of homogenous produce which looks attractive and has a long shelf life. Flavour is a very minor consideration. You need a knife to hull most of the strawberries they sell! English plums are almost non-existent. The big, fat red ones which are imported, are as tasty as cardboard soaked in water. The same few varieties of apples and pears seem to be offered all the year round.

There is great opportunity for a grower who is able to offer soft fruit and plums, picked when ripe and full of flavour, rather than having to be picked unripe and carted halfway round the world. Ripe plums have a very short shelf life; picked unripe they will eventually soften, but not be worth eating. There is one advantage in soft fruit being available in the supermarkets all year round. When they were seasonal the price received at the start of the season was much higher than later, so it was a big advantage to grow early fruit. Outdoor strawberries will ripen from June. If you wanted to start earlier, polytunnels would be necessary. This would mean having to have irrigation available; this, and the production of the material for the tunnels, all adds to the carbon footprint.

There were varieties of apples and pears ripening from July to late October. Beauty of Bath was an early variety. With storage facilities, it should be possible to sell well after Christmas. The orchard area could also support free range poultry and/or bee hives. A hive or two would, of course, be very useful for pollination.

To succeed with a smallholding today, it is necessary to enjoy hard physical work. I use the word 'enjoy' deliberately, as the results can be very rewarding. Gone are the days when there was a willing pool of labour to do the work for you. The descendants of the families who considered hop-picking to be their summer holiday, have probably flown off to the Costa del Sol. It is this lack of available labour which may cause the big growers to fall flat on their faces. English people are not prepared to do much hard work, in fact many are not capable of it. At present foreign workers are available but this may not last. It is a very different matter to harvest your own crops, which you have planned, planted and presented for sale, than simply the mindless picking of a crop in which you have no interest, and are not expected to have any interest. The subsequent production lines are no better. Some of the work would be an insult to a retarded monkey.

In the days when the grower parted with his produce at the farm gate, it didn't matter what his views of the public were, and whether he was a miserable character with a constant scowl. Now it matters a great deal. It is surprising what a genuine smile can achieve.

It is unlikely that you would be able to make 100% of your income from the holding. A recent survey of Farmers' Markets showed that only 12% of stall holders did this. In any case, another source of income is necessary while you are setting up.

Bearing the above in mind, running a smallholding can be a very rewarding and interesting way of life; far better than sitting in a stuffy office waiting to be made redundant.